Ein Prosit!

A practical guide to Oktoberfest

By Chris Harrison

Oktoberfest

It lasts for two weeks. Over five million people will visit. Nearly six million litres of beer will be drunk, dropped, or spilled on the tables while dancing. Visitors from across the world will eat more than half a million roast chicken, over a hundred oxen, and uncountable numbers of grilled sausages. There will be lederhosen as far as the eye can see, rollercoasters will light up the sky, thousands of guests will party the night away inside vast tents before going home to collapse, exhausted. Then they will get up, and do it all over again.

It is the greatest party on earth. And it happens every year.

Welcome to Oktoberfest.

Copyright ©

2014, 2015, 2017 Chris Harrison

Survival Page

Important German

Most people will speak English, but sometimes you need to get your point across with a bit of German. Here are a few of the most useful words and phrases which you'll need at Oktoberfest, right at the start for easy access.

English	German
Hi! My name is [name] and my hotel is at [address]. Please help me to find it!	Servus! Ich bin [name] und mein Hotel ist in der [address], Bitte helfen Sie mir, es zu finden!
Hey man!	Servus!
[one, two, three, four] beers thanks!	[ein, zwei, drei, vier] Bier bitte!
Is this seat free?	Ist hier noch frei?
I can't speak German, do you know English?	Ich kann kein Deutsch, können Sie Englisch?
Yes / No	Ja / Nein
Pity...	Schade...
Thanks	Danke
No worries	Passt scho'
Enjoy your meal	Mahlzeit / An Guadn
Fuck.	Himmiherrgottzagramentzefix-hallelujamilextamarsch-scheissglumpfaregts

Emergency numbers

If something goes wrong, it's best to have the important phone numbers close to hand. Here are a few of the more important ones.

Who are you calling?	Their phone number
Police	110
Fire / Ambulance	112
'Sichere Wiesn' security point	+49 (0)89 / 50 222 366
Aussie Embassy	+49 (0)30 880088-0
British Embassy	+49 (0)89 211090
Canadian Embassy	+49 (0)89 2199570
New Zealand Embassy	+49 (0) 172 7206 992
US Embassy	+49 (0)89 2888-0

Table of Contents

Introduction

Oktoberfest is easily the biggest party in the world. Every year almost six million people will visit the two-week, three-weekend long celebration of beer, delicious food, and Lederhosen. They will dance, drink, sing, and go home to tell all of their friends what an amazing time they had.

Everyone should visit Oktoberfest at least once in their lives – and if you are reading this book, chances are you agree. But though everyone has heard of Oktoberfest, there are a lot of things you need to know before you get there. Not the traditions and the history, though we will cover that too, but rather the **useful** things to know.

Useful things, such as:

- How do I get to the festival?
- Which tent is the best tent?
- How can I get a seat?
- What are the best things to eat? And drink?
- Which rollercoasters are the best?
- Where can I get those awesome outfits?

So, if you want to do Oktoberfest right: to get drunk like a German, to find those empty seats, discover the best tents, sing the *Fliegerlied* like a champion, and rock a pair of leather pants like a real Bavarian, then this is the book for you.

Read on, and learn the things you actually need to know!

An overview of this book

This book will provide you with the information you need in order to enjoy the perfect Oktoberfest visit. There are a lot of things to learn, so we have split everything up into several areas to make life easier. In order, we'll be covering:

Planning: What you need to know before you get to Oktoberfest. We'll be providing information such as the correct dates, how to get to Munich, the best days to go, opening hours, finding accommodation, and other important information.

The big day: Your visit to the best party in the world, Oktoberfest. Here we cover the best ways to get to the festival, how to choose the best tent and find a seat, various things you need to know inside the tents, and some information on costs and money.

Eating and drinking: The best part of the festival! Whether you are interested in beer or other drinks, snacks or full Bavarian meals, this section has you covered.

Rides: Not just a drinking festival, half of Oktoberfest is also given over to rides and stalls. Here we cover some of the traditional favourites.

After the music stops: Eventually the party has to end – or does it? Here we look at how to get home once the tents closed, and also where to go for some more partying.

Safety: Have a great time, but stay safe. This section covers important safety-related tips for all the visitors.

What to wear at Oktoberfest: Everyone recognises the Oktoberfest outfits, be they *Lederhosen* or *Dirndls*. This section will tell you where to get your own set, and what you should look out for.

History: Oktoberfest is a party with over 200 years of tradition behind it. Learn a bit about the history behind the drinking.

Wiesn songs and German words: There is a lot of music and a lot of dancing – and it is a pity if you don't know what's going on. These sections cover the most popular songs and a few useful terms you should know.

Mr Maß's words of wisdom

Nobody knows Oktoberfest like a talking glass of beer, so Mr Maß will also be here to provide quick tips and important information as we go along.

The serious part

Oktoberfest is fantastic, it's the biggest party in the world, and should be done by everyone at least once in their lives. But it's also a *lot of beer*, stronger than you're used to, and you can get very, very wasted. There is a line between have a fantastic party and getting hauled off by the police – or even getting hit and killed by a train, as has happened several times recently. The line is very easy to cross...

You'll probably be drunk. That's ok. Just don't be a **stupid** drunk.

Know what you're doing, stay with your buddies, don't skol the whole thing, definitely don't hit anyone with the glass, and don't be a bloody idiot. Be, in fact, responsible.

Planning your trip

Just turning up and getting a beer is certainly possible for locals, but tourists need to worry about accommodation, planning, getting there, etc. This section covers the things which you need to know before you get to Oktoberfest.

Where is Oktoberfest?

This is a very basic question but one which does occasionally trip people up. Oktoberfest is held in the city of Munich, itself located in the state of Bavaria which makes up the south-east corner of Germany. When travelling around the signs are, naturally enough, in German, and so you should look for *München, Bayern, Deutschland.*

Munich is one of the largest cities in Germany and is constantly growing thanks to its bustling economy and role as a high-tech hub. Despite this the city retains a relaxed attitude and small-town feel – helped in part by the law that no building can be taller than the *Frauenkirche* church, in the middle of the city.

The festival itself is located in the *Theresienwiese* Park, a large open area in the central-west part of Munich. As *Theresienwiese* is quite a mouthful, locals will usually just call it the *Wiesn* – you will often hear people say they are 'going to the Wiesn'.

On a clear day you can see all the way to the Alps

Reaching Munich

Munich is quite easy to reach by every form of travel. Most airlines offer flights into Munich Airport (*München Flughafen*), often direct within Europe although those coming from Australia or the United States will normally have to change at London, Frankfurt or Dubai. The airport has a fast rail link to the city and you can expect to get into the city centre within about 50 minutes by train, slightly longer by taxi or airport shuttle bus depending on traffic. Budget airlines will sometimes fly into Memmingen Airport, sometimes optimistically referring to it as 'Munich West'. Be aware that it is *very* west, being in a completely different city and about 110km away from Munich itself. If you fly in to Memmingen expect to need over an hour and a half to reach Munich proper.

Fast trains connect Munich to the rest of Europe, travellers will usually take the Inter-City Express (ICE) lines from Deutsche Bahn. All ICE lines will stop at the *München Hauptbahnhof* (Munich's main train station) and usually *München Ostbahnhof* ('Munich East', the second rail hub). The Hauptbahnhof in particular is very closely located, within walking distance of Oktoberfest and so arriving by train is a popular option.

A cheaper alternative to the train network are the long distance buses, many different companies now offer bus connections between various European cities and Munich. Buses usually offer free wireless internet and various snacks, though you will have less leg room than you would on the train system. Also be aware that the majority of buses will stop at *München ZOB*, the Central Bus Station, which is actually about half a kilometre west of the Hauptbahnhof. If you need to transfer and don't want to walk, simply take the train from the nearby Hackerbrücke station.

The last option is to simply drive to Munich, using the excellent German *Autobahn* (highway) network. Unfortunately Munich has some very impressive traffic jams, particularly around Oktoberfest when many of the roads are closed. Expect to be sitting around doing nothing for a while, and be sure that the hotel has their own parking.

The Inter-City Express fast trains connect Munich with other locations across all of Europe.

When is Oktoberfest?

For a start, Oktoberfest isn't really in October (German humour strikes again). Once upon a time it truly was an October-fest, but after a while everyone realised that the weather was much nicer a month or so earlier and so decided to shift it by a few weeks – Oktoberfest is now technically a Septemberfest. On the plus side, the change means that there is a much better chance of visiting on a sunny, blue-sky day. On the negative side, the inaccurate naming tends to catch a *lot* of people out, which means it is amusingly common to see tourists wandering around in mid-October wondering where the party is.

Luckily, there is always a backup plan for those who picked the wrong dates and arrived too late. Take the train to Stuttgart (about 2 hours away by fast train) and go visit the *Cannstatter Volksfest*, the second biggest beer festival in the world. Actually, you might want to do that regardless of whether you got to Oktoberfest or not – the party feeling is almost as good in Stuttgart as in Munich and you can keep the drinking spree going for a few more days.

But assuming that you are trying to get to the *real* beer festival, when should you go? The official rule is that Oktoberfest runs for three weekends (16 days in total) starting in September and finishing on the **first Sunday** in October. Unless, that is, the 16th

day is **before** October 3rd (German reunification day and a national holiday), in which case it will run for several days extra to make sure that it finishes on the 3rd.

Confused? Here's a simple table to help you sort everything out.

If the first Sunday in October is the...	Then Oktoberfest starts on Saturday, September the...	And ends on October the...	Which is a...
1st	16th	3rd	Monday
2nd	17th	3rd	Tuesday
3rd	18th	3rd	Sunday
4th	19th	4th	Sunday
5th	20th	5th	Sunday
6th	21st	6th	Sunday
7th	22nd	7th	Sunday

The best day to visit

You've planned ahead and you know when Oktoberfest is actually on. The next step is to decide *which day*. This is often very dependent on your other travel plans, but you should remember than many other people, both tourists and locals, will be aiming to visit the festival as well.

As such the busiest days will be the weekends, particularly on Saturdays (as everyone can sleep off the hangover on

Sunday). Lots of people in Europe fly in for a short drinking weekend on Friday, then head out on Sunday evening. Add the Munich local crowd (who also get weekends off) and you can already see the problem – a problem which only gets worse on sunny days when *everyone* decides that they may as well visit the Wiesn.

Weekends are busy, but the second weekend is the busiest of all. Informally known as Italian Weekend, large numbers of visitors from Italy will catch the bus up, get very drunk on Saturday night, and then catch the bus back. Tents are regularly packed by 9:30am on Italian Weekend and they rarely get any emptier – if you have to be there, come early! If you are planning a longer trip through Europe alongside your Oktoberfest visit, then your best approach is to visit on a weekday – the crowds are generally less and you have a better chance of getting a table through to mid-afternoon. The tent atmosphere will be slightly less party-oriented during the day – tents usually switch to the better songs in the afternoon rather than in the morning. However, from roughly 4pm onwards the place will be full of people and everyone will be dancing on tables by the end of the night, just as they would on the weekend. This of course leads to the question – how many times should you go?

The local tradition is to go three times – once with work, once with family, once with friends. As a visitor this doesn't really apply, but it's usually worth going at least twice – if nothing else because there is too much going on to see it all in one day. If you only have a few days then do your hard drinking on the first night, recover for a day, go back on the third night. Your liver will thank you.

While the general character of Oktoberfest is the same for the entire festival, there are a few 'special' days:

The first Saturday: When everything starts! While the tents open at the normal time, they will only start selling beer at 12 noon, the moment the first keg has been tapped by the mayor of Munich and who will shout out the traditional *O'zapft is!* –

Mr Maß's words of wisdom

It's usually not worth turning up before opening time. However, tents will fill up very quickly on weekends – especially a sunny Saturday. If you know it will be a beautiful weekend, get there early!

Impressively-decorated carriages are everywhere during the Oktoberfest parades

"the beer is tapped". The tents will be full long before then, so you may have a long period of waiting before your first beer. If that's too much stress for you, hang out outside and watch the mini-parade, where heavily-decorated horses pull carriages full of beer.

The first Sunday: This is when *the* parade happens, large enough to last for hours. It includes representatives from all the breweries, various hunting associations, random men cracking whips for fun, about a million different brass bands, and members of almost every *Verein* (club) in Munich. The parade will start from *Marienplatz* (the central square) and wind through the city on the way to *Theresien-wiese*. The parade is long and so the crowds are spread out, which means that it is usually easy to find a spot to watch.

The *first Sunday* and *second Monday* are the traditional 'Gay *Wiesn*' days, where traditionally most of Munich's queer scene will descend on one tent (Braürosl on Sunday, Fischer-Vroni on Monday). If you want to join then *go early*, it gets packed very fast.

The first Monday: Is usually a lot quieter than on the weekend. The first Monday is also more adult-focused, and those over 65 can get cheaper meals in the tents.

The first and second Tuesday: Both Tuesdays are considered 'family day'. This means that all of the rides and performances will cost less than they normally would, at least between 10am-7pm. If you are travelling with family, this is a good chance to enjoy the carnival side of Oktoberfest, others may simply enjoy riding the rollercoasters a few more times. Just remember that rollercoasters revert to full price later in the evening.

The first Thursday: Is the day for the traditional Oktoberfest church service. Begun in 1956 as a way to provide a religious service for the merchants and carnival-folk, it was later opened up to all comers. The service was traditionally held in the Hippodrom tent, but has since moved to Marstall. Entrance is free, service begins at 10am.

The middle weekend: Is popularly known as *Italian Weekend*, when hordes of Italians catch buses over the Alps to Munich. Normally they'll be at Oktoberfest from Saturday morning or so, party the whole way through, then depart, hungover and happy, on Sunday.

The last day: The last day of

Oktoberfest is usually a Sunday, though may be a Monday or Tuesday in some years. Regardless of the day, being there is a fantastic if crowded experience. Tents will celebrate the final songs by giving everyone sparklers or lights to wave around, the guests will all link arms and sing sadly as the night closes out, and everyone will feel a bit depressed that the party is over for another year. If you can manage it, definitely visit on the last day.

Italian Weekend

The middle (2nd) Oktoberfest weekend is now well-established as the 'Italian Weekend'. Nobody really knows why, but when that second Saturday morning comes around the vast majority of the crowd lining up outside the tent before opening will be from all sorts of Italian towns. This is a well-known fact to all the tent organisers, who often won't even bother with announcements in German on those mornings. It is also well-known to the city of Munich, who regularly invite representatives from the Italian *Polizia* to join their German counterparts on patrol throughout the grounds. Similarly there are usually a number of extra ambulances which will be crewed by Italian paramedics.

This is not to say that there are no non-Italians around on that day, but there is certainly a very high chance that anyone you meet will be Italian. This has pluses and minuses. On the plus side, you will have a great time and make a bunch of really outgoing new friends, friends which will definitely be up for partying on throughout the night (if they are still standing by that stage, at least). The minus is that it becomes much, much harder to find a seat on Italian weekend, even worse if you have a medium/large-sized group. Thus if Saturday is your only option you need to be lining up outside a tent by 8am, preferably outside one of the big ones such as Winzerer-Fähndl.

Italian weekend is normally concentrated on the Saturday. After a heavy night of partying, most of the heavily-hungover visitors will then jump on a coach on Sunday, spending a few hours enjoying the vomit-filled bus ride back over the Alps.

Mr Maß's words of wisdom

General tip: don't travel to Italy by bus on the Italian Weekend Sunday!

Opening hours

Opening hours are different depending on which day you are going and what you're intending to do.

At 8am, there will be a crowd of early drinkers standing around outside the tents and waiting to be let in. All of them will be tourists, or Munich locals with tourist friends. This may be a good idea on a sunny Saturday, other days aren't worth it.

The tents, realistically the main reason people go to Oktoberfest, will open a bit before 9-10am. Officially the opening hours (and the first beer serving) will be at 10 am on weekdays and 9 am on weekends. Realistically they will be open about 15 minutes before that so you can rush in. On the first Saturday, the tents will open but *no beer will be served until midday*, when the first keg is tapped.

Stalls (selling everything from toasted almonds to silly hats) will officially open at 9am on weekends and 10am on weekdays.

Rides (rollercoasters, slides, haunted houses, etc.) will open at 10am on all days but the first Saturday, when they will open at midday.

At 10:30pm the band will stop playing in the tents and

security will politely (and then less politely) encourage you to leave. No more beer will be served after this time, realistically servers will stop selling beer at about 10:20 or so. Some tents (such as Käfer) will stay open for longer, but you will have no chance of getting in at this time.

All stalls and rides will close down at midnight on Fridays and Saturdays, and at11:30pm on all other days.

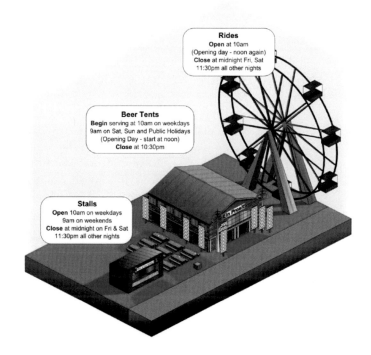

Yes, this means you can go on a rollercoaster after getting wasted. Yes, it is just as good an idea as it sounds.

There are roughly three drinking shifts throughout the day, starting at 9 am (tourists), lunchtime (lazy tourists, locals going for a long lunchbreak, and locals starting the party early), and 5 pm (everyone else). There will usually be a customer changeover between each of these shifts, and in fact this is where the tents make a lot of their money (as fresh, sober people will drink more in the next hour than the drunks they are replacing). Unfortunately this often means that waiters will heavily pressure you to drink continuously, and will sometimes enlist security to throw the slow-drinking groups out. To avoid this, make sure you always have a non-empty drink in your hand or on the table in front of you – you don't need to be drinking from it, it just needs to *look* as though you are.

If you do get in early, remember to drink at a reasonable rate. The party will run through until 10:30pm, while the best parts won't start until 5pm or so. Don't get so drunk in the first hour that

you have to miss the fun part!

Finding somewhere to stay

Actually finding a place to stay is probably one of the most difficult parts of planning your Oktoberfest visit. Hotels will regularly put their prices up to two or three times the non-Oktoberfest costs and free rooms will rapidly disappear. There are a few general things to remember when looking for your place:

Book early! Oktoberfest is not something that you can do spontaneously, because everyone else has the same idea. This is a major problem for backpackers and other people staying in hostels – the popularity of Oktoberfest means that hostel beds are booked out well in advance. Ideally you'll be planning your trip by the start of the year and will have booked by March at the latest. There will still be rooms free all the way through to September, but the amount you will pay for them will climb exponentially. Save your wallet, book early!

Sleep nearby. Staying in the vicinity of Theresienwiese will allow you to easily walk to and from the festival, but will come with a correspondingly high price tag. Although being able to stagger home is a massive plus, if you are stuck for a room then think about looking further away in the Munich public transport network. The easiest districts to reach are those connected on the subway lines U3/6 and U4/5 (both of which pass directly by Oktoberfest) or on the main S-bahn lines (which will require you to walk back to the Hauptbahnhof).

Try a share-house. The popularity of sharing platforms such as AirBnB has also reached Munich, with the result that a lot of people are offering rooms or beds in their apartments for a few nights. The prices are usually cheaper than a hotel and you can get some great locations – just be aware that people are less tolerant of you coming back drunk than hotel staff.

If you can't find anything in Munich which matches your budget, you can also look further out. The S-bahn network covers a vast number of suburbs and hotels, you can even go further out and stay in neighbouring Rosenheim if you want. Bear in mind that you will probably be cold and drunk when travelling home, thus a one hour train trip may not be the best option.

If you really want to go cheap, then you can camp outside Munich with either a tent or a caravan. This can either be great fun or a sleazy hell-hole, depending on weather, where you book, and how the neighbours are – so you really take your chances here. As with hotels, camping prices go up during the Oktoberfest period – though they remain much cheaper than a real hotel or hostel. Caravans aren't allowed within the immediate surroundings of *Theresienwiese*, you will have to find somewhere outside the inner city to park.

Mr Maß's words of wisdom

Accommodation is probably the biggest difficulty when trying to visit Oktoberfest. Book early and save yourself a lot of frustration later on!

Planning ahead: important information to know

There is a range of important information which you need to know before you arrive at the festival. Here's a quick rundown of the most important things.

What to wear

The Oktoberfest-season is roughly early autumn, which means it's a confusing mix of warm and cold. There will be sunny days where you can happily sit outside with your beer and soak up some UV. Then there are other days where clouds will cover the sky and rain will force you inside before midday.

Nights can get bitter cold and so you may want to think about bringing some sort of jacket along. The disadvantage of doing this is that the tent is warm and there are rarely good places to store the jacket – most people hang it through the table legs but this will often end up soaked in beer by the end of the night. The truly prepared will bring a plastic bag along to keep it dry. Most other people will simply accept the cold or the beery shower.

Beyond that, there is no real dress code at the Wiesn. Despite what you see on TV; there are plenty of people who turn up in jeans and t-shirts. However if you really want to fit in, think about buying a set of *Lederhosen* or a *dirndl* – see the later chapter in this book for more information on how to go about it. If you're still at home then it may be worth looking online to see what is available (eBay and Amazon have a surprising amount to buy, just skip the Halloween versions). Otherwise you can wait until you get to Munich proper, there are thousands of options in the city.

Visiting with children

Despite what you would think, Oktoberfest is actually quite a child-friendly place to visit. Around half of Theresienwiese is dedicated to rides, rollercoasters, carnival attractions and food – and all of it will keep kids highly entertained for hours. Keep in mind that both Tuesdays are considered 'Family Day', rides and stalls will offer a number of discounts for children and families.

Children usually find the

main tents incredibly boring and so you may have issues with keeping them entertained if you bring them along. To make things more complicated, baby strollers and large backpacks aren't allowed on the festival grounds due to security reasons – keep this in mind when packing for the day.

If you are looking for something more relaxing than the usual rides, try taking the family to the *Familien-Platzl*, a relatively quiet spot on the east side of Theresienwiese. With a number of calmer rides and a miniature Biergarten, it is a good way to catch a moments' breath. Another good option is the *Oide Wiesn*, a historical reenactment of the original Oktoberfest, complete with old-style rides and entertainment.

The rules regarding attendance for children and teenagers are significantly easier than an equivalent festival in Australia or the United States:

- The drinking age is 16. Anyone younger than this isn't allowed alcohol, even if their parents are present. Teenagers between 16 and 18 are allowed to drink beer but nothing stronger. Over 18, anything goes.

- Anyone under 16 needs to have a parent present at *all times* when inside the tents and any time *after 8pm* outside the tents.

- Kids under 6 must leave the tents at 8pm, even when accompanied by their parents, but can still hang around in the outside sections and fairground.

Visiting with a wheelchair

Oktoberfest is in general suitable for guest with wheelchairs or other mobility aids. There are usually special tables with better access set aside in the tents, though you won't be able to get up to the balconies (as no tent has an elevator installed). The main boulevards outside are relatively flat and paved over, although they have fairly deep gutters running across the path which may be a surprise.

Gay?

Like most German cities, Munich has a strong 'gay-friendly' atmosphere. Oktoberfest, despite the traditional roots, continues this tradition. There are two locations which are considered to be the unofficial-yet-traditional 'gay Oktoberfest': in the Bräurosl on the first Sunday, and in Fischer-Vroni on the second Monday. Both events are extremely popular (in particular the Bräurosl) which means that the tents will be jam-packed before midday. If you want a seat, go early.

The outfits and general dress-code is much more varied than the typical tents, with everything from sparkling costumes through to deeply traditional *Tracht*. If you want to dress up or across, keep in mind that, although girls in *Lederhosen* are a common sight in the general Oktoberfest grounds, guys in a *Dirndl* are not. You will probably get some stares while on the general grounds and security in other tents may assume that you are part of a stag/bucks' night and so refuse you entry. Just explain politely and everything should be fine.

The after-*Wiesn* party will usually move to the *Glockenbachviertel* (head east to *Sendlinger Tor* and then south). *Glockenbachviertal* is jam-packed with excellent bars and also doubles as Munich's unofficial 'gay district' – there are a number of gay bars scattered around and the atmosphere is very relaxed (the area also hosts the Pink Christmas Market, well worth a look if you are back in December). The best party location changes from year to year, so the easiest way to find one is simply to ask a local. The tents involved in the 'gay Oktoberfest' tend to have a much higher proportion of locals than others, which means you have a much better chance of getting good tips.

On the day of your visit

You've arrived at the festival! Hopefully all of the planning went well and it's now just a matter of enjoying yourself for the day. This chapter covers some of the most important things you will need to keep in mind on the big day, including getting to Oktoberfest, choosing the best tent, managing to find a seat, and other important information.

Getting to and from Theresienwiese

Theresienwiesn is quite well connected via public transport. The best option is usually to arrive via the underground (*U-bahn*) system, as you can either take the U4/U5 line to exit at *Theresienwiesn* or *Schwanthalerhöhe* stations or take the U3/U6 and get out at *Poccistraße* or *Goetheplatz* stations. Walking time to the festival grounds will range from ten seconds (Theresienwiese station) to about ten minutes (Goetheplatz).

Visitors coming from further out will usually take the S-bahn and then exit at the Hauptbahnhof. This is then an easy fifteen minute walk to reach the north end of the festival grounds. Regardless of whether you take the U-bahn or S-bahn, there will be signs pointing out the correct direction (and a literal stream of people walking there, you cannot miss it).

If you dislike walking then it is also possible to get a lift via taxi to the grounds, though there will be serious traffic issues for the last kilometre or so. Munich also has a number of pedal-powered rickshaws (invariably driven by students) which will pick people up from various train stations and drop them off at Oktoberfest.

All of these options are available when you want to leave Oktoberfest as well. The only downside is that tens of thousands of people will be leaving at the same time, as every tent stops the party at 10:30pm. This makes getting onto the U-bahn at Theresienwiese a nightmare and so you are much better off trying to walk to a different stop. Rickshaws are also very popular within the local area – they are both fast and able to avoid most of the traffic jams.

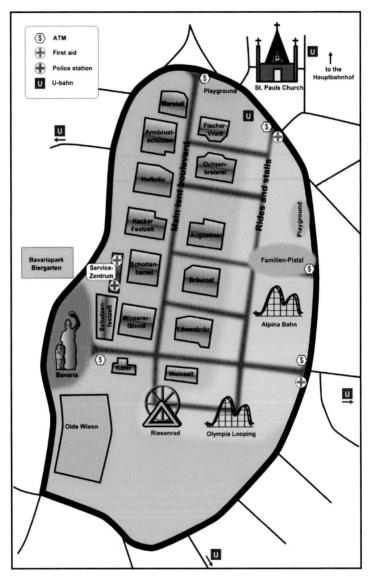

The Oktoberfest layout at Theresienwiese

Alternatively, go and find a bar in the vicinity and keep the party going for a while longer – the majority of the crush is over by 11:30pm on most nights.

One thing you should *not* do is try to drive yourself to Oktoberfest. There is essentially no parking available for non-residents, your car will be towed, and you will be stuck in traffic for hours. And then the police will pick you up for drunk driving when you try to leave. *Don't drive to Oktoberfest!*

Getting into the grounds

Although the *Wiesn* used to be completely open, terrorist concerns in recent years have led to the addition of a fence around the entire grounds. This means that everyone will need to enter through one of the main gate areas on each side, note that police will check if you are carrying large handbags or the like.

Although there are gates, there is no admission charge to enter the *Wiesn* – don't fall for someone trying to sell you tickets. A ticket is required to visit the *Oide Wiesn*, a recreation of the historical Oktoberfest, this will cost you a few Euro and

can be bought at the clearly obvious ticket counters. Tickets of a sort do exist for the tents – people who have made reservations will also get a voucher for ten Euro or so to be spent on food and drinks. You may find scalpers selling these around the place and they usually represent a good deal – just make sure the tickets are for the correct tent and year.

Kids are allowed in the tents, though they have to be with an adult and (obviously) can't drink alcohol. The age limit for buying beer is 16, for 'hard' drinks 18. Security does check people, so always bring ID just in case, (passports will fit into *Lederhosen* pockets, so no excuses). Bags will sometimes be searched, and they usually confiscate bottles of water, etc.

Choosing a tent

There are six big Munich breweries allowed to sell beer at the Oktoberfest (Augustiner, Hacker-Pschorr, Löwenbräu, Paulaner, Spaten, and Hofbräu). Each tent will be aligned with one of these, selling nothing but that brewery's beer. Many people say that Augustiner and Paulaner have the best Oktoberfest beer, realistically most visitors will not notice the fine differences and it is usually more important to choose a tent based on other factors.

There are 14 'major' tents to choose from, as well as a number of smaller ones which specialise in meals or snacks. The majority of visitors will go directly for the large tents, as these represent the typical 'Oktoberfest feeling'. All tents tend to have a similar party atmosphere, though differences definitely exist as described below. The most popular tents are usually Hacker, Hofbräu, and Winzerer-Fähndl, though you will have a good time in almost all of them.

The major *Wiesn* tents are as follows...

Marstall

Seating for:	*3200 inside, 1000 outside*
Colours:	*Yellow, red, bit of green*
Brewery:	*Spaten-Franziskaner*

The newcomer to the scene, thanks to some back-room drama. This location was, up until 2014, where the Hippodrom tent was – a favourite location for celebrities, fashionable types, and, well, people who think that they are fashionable. Unfortunately the glitz and glamour was also a cover for some allegedly dodgy tax dealings, and in punishment the city took away the licence. The spot was, naturally, prime real estate and so was quickly bought up by another catering group. To continue the horse-related theme they named the tent *Marstall* (an old German word for a lord's stables) and stuck some horse-related decoration here and there.

Marstall caters to the same general audience that Hippodrom did. This means that they are much pickier about who they let in (i.e. drunken tourists usually won't have a chance) and will often have staff lead you to a seat rather than allowing you to freely wander. Marstall is perhaps best thought of as a location

Marstall continues the horse-related theme of Hippodrom.

for *being seen* rather than a location to get drunk and party hard – as such it really isn't the best choice for the majority of visitors.

Those with a yearning to check out Hippodrom can still find it at the Munich Frühlingsfest (spring festival), although as the name suggests this is quite a few months away. Occasionally the tent will also be set up during Oktoberfest, albeit in a location north of the Hackerbrücke railway station. They do stay open significantly later than the main Oktoberfest tents, so it may be an option for some.

Armbrustschützenzelt

Seating for:	*5850 inside, 1600 outside*
Colours:	*Green and white*
Brewery:	*Paulaner*

Armbrustschützenzelt is in the middle as far as Oktoberfest tents go – it is neither as classy as Marstall nor as touristy as Hofbräu. Because of this it tends to attract a more relaxed crowd, though the beer, food and party are usually as good as the Wiesn average. A major plus of this more relaxed approach is that the tent will have open seats for much longer than other tents – if you have a large group or are attending later in the day then it can be worth going here directly to find a spot.

An *Armbrustschütze* is a crossbow archer, and the tent follows this theme by having a number of (fake) animal heads mounted on the walls, while a giant, somewhat possessed-looking wild boar stands guard over the entrance. To complete the theme, a crossbow competition is held in the attached shooting range (sadly only for the experts, if you want to shoot something yourself then you will have to head outside to the fairgrounds).

Armbrustschützenzelt is relatively easily spotted by the big tower and sundial at the front.

Hofbräu Festhalle

Seating for:	*6900 inside, 3000 outside*
Colours:	*Blue and white*
Brewery:	*Hofbräu*

Hofbräu is probably the best-known of the Munich breweries internationally, having spent quite a lot of money getting their name into the general consciousness. This can also be seen at Oktoberfest, where the majority of people in the Hofbräu tent will be international visitors – most commonly Aussies and Americans. Actual Germans are fairly rare at Hofbräu, partly due to the impression that it's full of completely wasted foreigners.

Hofbräu is very, very popular, and its popularity with tourists in particular (who tend to start earlier than locals) means that there are queues before opening every day. Having said that, the party atmosphere is excellent, the band will play *Wiesn*-hits as early as they can, and you are guaranteed to be very drunk by about 11am or so, easy.

The famous Hofbräu

Because of this the Hofbräu tent tends to divide opinions. If you want a good party with other foreigners, it is a good place to visit. If you want a good party with locals, you should look into one of the other tents. Whatever you decide on, you should at least walk through once to get an impression of the place.

Mr Maß's words of wisdom

You will find branches of the Hofbräuhaus across the entire world, from Australia to Japan. This global reach is exactly why everyone thinks of Hofbräu first when they think of Oktoberfest.

Hacker-Festzelt

Seating for: *6.900 inside, 2400 outside*

Colours: *The inside is painted: a blue sky and white clouds*

Brewery: *Hacker-Pschorr*

Hacker is a local favourite in Munich and is considered to have one of the better party-scenes. Because of this it tends to fill up much faster than the other tents and so you really need to be early if you want to get a spot – especially if there are more than two of you. What does this mean in practice? Ideally before 3-5 pm on a weekday, before 10-12 am on a weekend, and possibly before 7 am on Italian Weekend.

The tent is known as *Der Himmel der Bayern* – which usually translates as the Bavarian Heaven (or, for the less poetic, the Bavarian Sky). Painted bright blue and with bouncy clouds hanging everywhere, the interior decoration makes the tent feel very open even when packed full of partygoers.

In general Hacker is usually a great first choice for people visiting. The beer is good, the music is usually more upbeat and party-like than the other tents, and the crowd is both local and young.

Schottenhamel

Seating for: *6000 inside, 4000 outside*

Colours: *Blue*

Brewery: *Spaten-Franziskaner*

Schottenhamel is best known for being the tent where the very first beer of the entire festival is served. As the stroke of 12 noon on the first Saturday the *Bürgermeister* (Mayor) of Munich will get up on stage and hammer the tap into the first keg. How many strokes it actually takes to get beer is a matter of much gossip, very few things boost a politician's popularity like tapping the keg in two hits. In any case, once the beer is flowing he will shout out

O'zapft is! (it's tapped!) and the festival is on.

Those who are not the Bürgermeister will have to wait a few more minutes to get their beer, but in general every tent will start serving alcohol the moment that the keg is tapped (admittedly, it can take up to 30 minutes before the service people actually get to you with the beer, but that's just part of the Oktoberfest fun).

After the first day (in which all of the local politicians will be represented) Schottenhamel becomes a relatively normal tent. A large section is usually set aside for *Studentenverbindungen*, a German equivalent to frat houses, which makes the crowd relatively young in comparison (although the usual *Studentenverbindung* member is often much more politically conservative that their frat-house equivalent).

Winzerer-Fähndl ("Paulaner")

Seating for: *8450 inside, 2450 outside*

Colours: *Yellow and white*

Brewery: *Paulaner*

Blessed with a name that is exceptionally hard for English-speakers to say, almost everyone simply takes the easy option and calls it the 'Paulaner' tent after the brewery it's associated with. The tent is very easy to recognise thanks to a giant, rotating beer Maß on top of a tower outside – something which can be seen from almost every point of the Wiesn.

Winzerer-Fähndl is easily the biggest tent, able to fit over eight thousand people inside.

Despite this, the bright colours and open-plan mean that it never really feels crowded. Beyond this the tent was the first to bring in *really* handy nets under the tables which you can stuff your jacket into. Although this sounds somewhat pointless, it stops the inevitable beer spills from soaking into your clothes (there are very few things as bad as putting on a jacket soaked in cold beer, and then

Yes, that rotating Maß

going out into the German night). Use the nets if they are there!

Thanks to its size, Winzerer-Fähndl is one of the best.options for large groups – particularly if they head up the back of the tent, where there are often entire tables free through into the afternoon. As with most of the tents, the real party atmosphere will start from around 5pm or so.

Schützen-Festzelt

Seating for:	*5440 inside, 1400 outside*
Colours:	*Green, yellow and red*
Brewery:	*Löwenbräu*

The Schützen-Festzelt is a middle-sized tent which is located off the main boulevard, being just next to the Bavaria statue (which, in case you haven't noticed it, is the really big bronze woman/lion combo towering over the hill).

Although the location has been occupied by Schützen for a long time, the actual tent is relatively new, having been completely redone in 2004.

The Schützen-Festzelt is best known for their Spanferkl, a roast piglet on a stick, (or at least slices of meat from the roast). Spanferkl is definitely worth ordering if you are there it is both a delicious meal and something which is essentially impossible to find in stalls or other locations outside the Schützen-Festzelt tent.

The Schützen Festzelt is slightly off the main boulevard, directly behind Winzerer-Fähndl

Käfer Wiesn-Schänke

Seating for: *1000 inside, 1900 outside*

Colours: *Wood-based decoration*

Brewery: *Paulaner*

Käfer is a fairly well-known supplier of gourmet food and high-level catering in the Munich area, and they take this general approach into their Oktoberfest tent, the Käfer Wiesn-Schänke. Usually considered the 'gourmet' tent, they aim for an older and richer crowd and usually attract a higher proportion of famous and powerful guests (this ranges from politicians through to sportsmen such as the FC Bayern team).

This focus means that it is a very different experience to the other tents, less of a party atmosphere and more of a social event. There is a heavy focus on upmarket *Tracht*, which means that the usual tourist-specials will stand out more than usual. Assuming you can even get in, as many tables are reserved and the security is quite picky about who can enter.

Like the Weinzelt, it stays open later than the other tents (past midnight, in fact). However, it is *very unlikely* that you will manage to get in after the other tents close, it usually makes more sense to go straight to an after-*Wiesn* party elsewhere in Munich.

The food is, naturally, excellent, although you will definitely be paying a premium compared to the usual fare.

This applies to everything within the tent, actually – if you do manage to get in then expect to be giving out significantly more money that you would otherwise plan to on a 'typical' Oktoberfest visit..

Weinzelt

Seating for:	*1900 inside, 600 outside*
Colours:	*Wood-based decoration*
Brewery:	*Wine from all over the place, and Weißbier from Paulaner*

As you would expect from a name like 'Weinzelt', the focus of this tent is wine. As with Käfer it targets an older and more laid-back crowd, offering not only a wide array of wines but a number of other gourmet meals. The furniture is more solid wood than the rickety tables of most tents, and it takes much longer before everyone is dancing on the banks.

As with Käfer, the Weinzelt is allowed to stay open later than the majority of tents, the band will play until midnight or so instead of 10:30pm. However the bouncers will become extremely picky after the other tents close and so you have very little chance of getting in. If you want to experience the Weinzelt properly, try to go early on a weekday when there are less reservations – just remember that you need to behave slightly better than the usual Oktoberfest visitor. If you can manage that, feel like avoiding the crowds and want to have a chilled-out day, definitely give the Weinzelt a try.

Löwenbräu

Seating for:	*5700 inside, 2800 outside*
Colours:	*Yellow*
Brewery:	*Löwenbräu*

Directly across from the Winzerer-Fähndl, Löwenbräu

is quite easy to find – it's just a matter of walking to the giant lion perched on a tower, drinking beer. To make it even easier, the lion will roar every couple of minutes to make sure you are paying attention to it. Why a lion? *Löwen* are 'lions', thus it is the tent for the Lions' Brewery.

The Löwenbräu tent is a good option for sunny days. The interior is quite light so you won't get the 'cave' effect which some other tents have. They also have an outdoors section which is amazingly popular, one which is definitely worth sitting in for a couple of hours on a sunny

A close up of the Löwenbräu lion shows him to be somewhat horrified by his drinking problem

day. Just be aware that the temperature will drop significantly once the sun goes down, so bring a jacket if you are planning to be outside later.

Pschorr-Bräurosl

Seating for:	*6220 inside, 2200 outside*
Colours:	*Blue and yellow*
Brewery:	*Hacker-Pschorr*

The Bräurosl is a solid fixture at Oktoberfest, one which has been managed by the same family for around seven generations (I like to imagine the kids growing up with tiny little beer-hall cubby houses). The name is meant to come from the original brewery owner's

daughter, and it's continued on as the official title of the tent yodeller (yes, Bräurosl has an official yodeller).

If you are ok with the occasional yodel, it is a nice tent with a good party atmosphere. Do be aware that it hosts the extremely popular *Rosa Wiesn* (the gay and lesbian Wiesn party) on the first Sunday, which means that it will be absolutely packed well before midday.

Augustiner-Festhalle

Seating for:	*6000 inside, 2500 outside*
Colours:	*Green*
Brewery:	*Augustiner*

Augustiner is generally considered one of the best breweries in Munich, with the dark-blue beer crate being a common site at picnics and riverside barbeques. The quality of the beer continues into Oktoberfest, where the tent still serves beer from the traditional *Hirschen* – wooden barrels with a capacity of about 200 litres.

With good beer and a friendly atmosphere, the Augustiner tent is a good all-around option. It has a reputation as a 'family' tent, especially on Tuesdays (family day, when all the rides are slightly cheaper), however as in all tents the kids need to leave at 8pm and the party will kick off with the same level of drunkenness as everywhere else.

Ochsenbraterei

Seating for:	*5900 inside, 1500 outside*
Colours:	*Blue and white*
Brewery:	*Spaten*

As you walk up to the entrance of the Ochsenbraterei you'll notice a giant, rotating, plastic ox on a spit just over the main doors. This should be a pretty clear hint as to the tent theme – various meals made from oxen. There are also the usual Bavarian meals available, but the beef is both exceptionally tasty and somewhat of a rarity at Oktoberfest (where chicken and pig tend to predominate) and so you should give it a try if you can. Alongside this is the usual good-quality beer and party atmosphere from about mid-afternoon onwards.

Beyond their delicious meals, the tent owners make a point of supporting local Bavarian farmers, using organic suppliers and running the location with renewable energy. If these are important factors to you then you may want to look into showing your support to the Ochsenbraterei.

Fischer-Vroni

Seating for:	*2700 inside, 700 outside*
Colours:	*Blue and yellow*
Brewery:	*Augustiner*

Fischer-Vroni focuses on fish, in particular the *Biergarten* favourite of *Steckerlfisch*: grilled-fish-on-a-stick. If you're a fan of fish, this place is fantastic, whether you'll be eating inside the tent or in the open-air section. If you hate fish, of course, you should go somewhere else – although all the usual meals are available you'll still be smelling fish around the place.

The tent is relatively new, having been in its current location since 1998. Somewhat less popular than the other tents, it takes a lot longer for all of the tables to fill up. Because of this it makes an excellent choice for larger groups or those who have turned up late on a sunny weekend. As long as you like fish, that is.

Oide Wiesn

Seating for:	*Multiple tents*
Colours:	*Varies*
Brewery:	*Varies*

The Oide Wiesn isn't really a tent, it's more a collection of tents within a fenced-off section of the Wiesn. Originally put together to celebrate the 200th anniversary in 2010, the

Oide Wiesn is designed as a recreation of how Oktoberfest used to be, when Munich had less than 100,000 inhabitants and everyone rode their horse and carriage to the paddock outside the city where the festival was to be held. There are restored, classic rides; gypsy fortune tellers; traditional dances in the tents, and when you order a beer it comes in *Tonkrüge*, the big stone mugs, rather than that fancy glass stuff.

It costs a couple of euro to enter the grounds, which tends to put off a lot of people. This entry cost combined with the fact that no tourists really know about it means that the Oide Wiesn is usually a more local crowd. The Oide Wiesn also tends to be less crowded and so it can often be a good place to check out if everywhere else is jam-packed (this applies even on Saturday evenings and closing night). The tents will play their own music rather than the usual *Wiesn*-hits, not only are the bands usually quite good but you will get a break from constantly doing the *Fliegerlied* dance again and again.

The Oide Wiesn shares a space with the agricultural show and is not set up eve-ry year like the other tents. A lot of back-door politicking is going on to determine whether the event becomes a permanent fixture or not. Because of this the easiest way to plan is to look it up online before you arrive – alternatively you can simply walk over there: if there's nothing but a carpark... come back next year.

Inside the tents

Finding a seat

Finding a seat is easily the most annoying part of the entire *Wiesn*. You won't get served if you aren't sitting (or standing) on a bench, which means that actually finding a spot is extremely important. Unfortunately everyone else is also trying to find a place at the same time, which means that there is a lot of competition. Actually finding a spot for you and your friends can be an absolute nightmare on busy days.

Mr Maß's words of wisdom

It can be difficult, but you will find a seat eventually. Don't get frustrated and just keep looking!

There are several different things to keep in mind when seat hunting, but most of them boil down to four main rules: split up, go early, target tables where everyone is wasted, and don't be too fussy about the tent. Let's look at these in order:

Split up

One or two people will never have a problem finding a seat. Find a table which is slightly spaced out, ask if they can shuffle along slightly so that you can fit. If they say no, move to the next table and ask. Eventually someone will say yes and then you are in.

If you have 3-5 people, then things get more difficult, very few occupied tables will have space for a medium group to drop down next to them. They will, however, usually have space for two people. Thus you should split the group and wander separately, in pairs, to try and find a spot. Once one pair has located a place, they can slowly call the others in the group over to join them. This act of invading a table is surprisingly effective in most circumstances.

This is of course also a danger for your group. Once you have a spot, don't lose it to new people! Take turns to go to the toilet, actively block 'small' groups which want to join you, try to take up more space than you need. Defend your table at all costs!

Bigger groups will usually need to follow the same approach, assuming that no empty tables can be found. It normally takes longer to join the group up again but this approach is equally effective. I have successfully gotten tables for groups of about 20 in the past, but it took a lot of searching and slow combining of smaller groups.

A word of warning for those who are shifting to join the larger group: finish your drink *before you move.* Bringing a drink with you is the equivalent of refusing to buy a drink at the new table. This reduces the amount which you spend on drinks at that table and thus reduces the earnings of the waiter assigned to that row – which in turn makes them angry. This can in turn lead to your entire group being thrown out of the tent (as indeed I've seen many times). Finish your drink before you move!

Go early

As mentioned earlier, there are roughly three drinking shifts throughout the day, starting at 9 am (tourists), lunchtime (lazy tourists, locals

going for a long lunchbreak, and locals starting the party early), and 5 pm (everyone else). This format applies on weekdays but usually breaks down on weekends, where you will expect the first visitors at 9am (tourists and locals) and then midday (tourists and locals who slept in). If you want the best chance of finding a seat, you should come before these peak times.

What does this mean?

On a weekday, you can usually get a seat if you arrive around 2-3pm. At this point the evening crowd have not yet arrived, while the morning crowd are drunk and ready to go home. Any time after 5pm will be increasingly difficult.

On a weekend, you should arrive before midday – particularly on a Saturday. Later times will still work, but you will find it harder and harder to find a free section. On sunny days the tents will often be closed by 1pm, thus you should aim to get in around 10am.

On Italian Weekend the tents will be jam packed by 10am. Either come very early (before 8-9am) or come later in the day when the early drinkers are starting to go home.

If you do get in early, remember to drink at a reasonable rate. The party will run through until 10:30pm, while the best parts won't start until 5pm or so. Don't get so drunk in the first hour that you have to miss the fun part!

Target tables with drunks

As mentioned before, waiters like fresh drinkers. People who have been drinking for a while will usually buy less beer and so are less profitable than those who have just arrived. You can use this to your advantage by targeting tables where most people are drunk.

First, find a table where the group is already quite wasted. The ideal group looks drunk and has at least one person who is 'just resting' their head on the table. These are inevitably tourists who went all-out and forgot that Oktoberfest beer is stronger than the normal brew. Say hi! They will undoubtedly speak English and will probably be friendly enough to let you sit down with them.

You will often notice that your new drunken friends will slowly give up and decide to go home (hopefully without vomiting on the table). This process can often be hurried along slightly by dropping hints to the waiter – about how you have several fresh friends waiting to party, for example. As the old table members leave, there will be ever-more space for your group.

Don't be too picky

Tents will get full and then close, this is a natural part of Oktoberfest. *When* they fill up, however, depends on how popular the tent is. Places which everyone wants to get into (such as Hacker for locals, Hofbräu for tourists) will fill to capacity quite quickly. By contrast, less popular tents (Fischer-Vroni, Armbrustschützenzelt, Käfer) or the very large tents (such as Winzerer-Fähndl) will take much longer to reach that point. If you know it's going to be a popular day, or you have a bigger group, it might be worth targeting one of the latter tents. You may not get into your 'dream tent', but you will be just as drunk by the end of the night.

Changing tents

In general you should plan to

find a seat and then stay there for the entire evening. Despite the advantages and disadvantages of each tent listed above, the general party atmosphere will be good regardless of the tent you choose – as long as you stay until closing. All tents will switch to party music in the afternoon, all will be full of people dancing on the benches and falling over by the end. As a rule of thumb, you should stay wherever you find a spot.

Having said that, sometimes you will want to change tents – perhaps you only have a few hours and want to get the best party, perhaps you really, really hate the smell of fish. Swapping tents is just a matter of getting up and walking to the next one. However, each tent will get steadily more crowded as the day goes on (eventually being closed completely) and it will become increasingly hard to find a free spot. This is particularly relevant if you are a large group, singles and pairs will be able to move much more easily. If you know that you are going to move, move early – don't wait until 10pm to try and get the perfect seat.

Finding your friends

Once you are inside, you will want to meet up with your friends. This is actually more difficult that you would expect, the tent is very loud and mobile coverage is often overwhelmed by the sheer number of connections involved. In general you want to stick to text-based communication – think SMS or instant messaging.

Each table will be in a certain numbered row, the row number (*Reihe*) is written on a sign attached to the beams, well above head height. Use these to communicate where you are – you can also use basic descriptions like 'near the band' or 'near the guys' toilet'. Some tents will clearly engrave the table number into the surface as well, your friends can always ask the waiters where they should look.

The weather problem

You will have noticed in the Tent section that a number of places are outside in the Biergarten. These are fantastic on the warm days, when sunshine, blue skies, and cold beer combine to make a perfect day. Unfortunately Oktoberfest also has its fair share of cold, grey, rainy days, days when no-one wants to sit outside and get miserably wet. The outcome of this is that the tents will fill up much faster on wet days than sunny ones – everyone wants to be inside, naturally enough.

What does this mean for you? Check the weather forecast before you go for the day. If it is going to be a cold, rainy day, *go earlier* than you normally would. Once you are inside then the weather doesn't matter, but there are few things worse than being stuck in a queue outside in the rain while everyone else is partying away indoors.

What happens when the tent is closed?

A lot of people want to attend Oktoberfest, and most of those want to get into the tents. This leads to crowding, especially on weekends, and thus the tents will often be closed to prevent even more overcrowding. It is easy to spot when this happens – there will be a big security guy standing in front of a closed door or barricade telling people to go away (occasionally the low tech version will occur, and there will be a sign saying 'closed').

There are a couple of options at this point.

Go elsewhere. You can simply go to another tent – there are plenty of them and it is rare that all are closed. Alternatively you can simply spend a bit of time in the outdoor section while waiting for the tent to open back up again, something which usually happens after an hour or two.

Try the back entrance. You can walk around to one of the back entrances (the ones which aren't on the main boulevard), as these are often open for longer. Be aware that the entrance for reservations will require actual proof (i.e. a tent pass) and the smokers' entrance usually uses stamps to keep track of people leaving and returning. If you don't have these then stick to the general entrances.

Ask nicely. You can ask security (very nicely) if you can go in. This probably won't work, especially if you don't know any German, but it never hurts to ask.

Ask 'very' nicely. You can ask security (very, very nicely) by, how shall we put this, including the prospect of financial remuneration. Although Germany prides itself on being generally free of corruption this is one case where bribery will, sadly, work in your favour. Bear in mind you still won't have a seat in the tent, that part is your problem.

Drink outside. If the tent is completely closed, then why not have a drink outside while you are waiting? Almost all of the tents have an outdoor section that is in general a pretty nice place to spend a few hours. The two disadvantages are the lack of live music and earlier closing times (not much earlier though). However neither of these are particularly important on a sunny day and so the outdoor section is a fantastic spot to spend a bit of time before trying to get into the main tent. This is, naturally, not a good option if it starts raining.

Bavariapark Biergarten. If you have tried all the options above and can't get into any of the tents, then try the 'last resort' option. Head to the *Bavariapark Biergarten* (hidden away in the forest behind the big bronze statue of Bavaria) and get yourself a drink. The *Bavariapark Biergarten* is close and yet relatively unknown - most people outside of Munich have never heard of it. However there are plenty of seats, it's easy to find a spot for your group, there is often live music throughout the day, and the beer is about €2 cheaper than in the tents. The biergarten is a great place to spend a few hours before wandering back to Oktoberfest proper.

Mr Maß's words of wisdom

Above all, don't get stressed! It may take a while, but you'll find a spot in the tents, and after the first glass you'll forget you were ever annoyed.

Reserved seats

A lot of the benches are set up for reservations, usually starting from 5 pm or so. You'll spot them easily as they're the empty ones with little signs saying *Reservierung* or *Reserviert.* While it is *theoretically* possible for a visitor to get a reserved table, in reality it is basically impossible for most people and the reservations will be snapped up within a few days after release. You can try contacting the tent directly at the start of the year to see if anything is free, but chances are fairly low. If you are staying at a high-class hotel in Munich then try asking the concierge, sometimes they will have a few reservations which can be passed on.

In general, however, the best chance 'regular' visitors have at a reservation is to buy it from someone else. You can find these offered online, although they are usually (a) dodgy, (b) very overpriced and (c) often scams which will be thrown out when you get to the tent. If you are going to try it, be very careful about who you buy from and know the risks going in.

Reserved tables also come with vouchers for food or drink (usually as a set value, so €10, etc.). Sometimes people with reservations can't use the voucher itself and so sell them to others in the tent at a discount. This is very often a good deal, but you will need to be sure that the vouchers you are buying are for the *current* Oktoberfest, not last years'.

Lastly, although tables will be reserved in the tents it is pos-

sible to sit there and order a drink. You will have to move before the reservation begins, so the waiters usually get pushy around 4:30pm. This can sometimes be a good option if you are just looking for a few drinks, but runs the risk that all of the better spots will be gone by the time you have to move.

Dancing

As the night rolls on and the party gets better, more and more people will get up on the benches to dance. This is perfectly fine, completely expected, and you should definitely do it as well.

Just keep a simple rule in mind: dance on the *benches*, never dance on the *table*. Security will quickly throw you out if you get up and dance on the table, no-one will care if you dance on the bench. You can often get away with putting one foot on the table for balance, but be prepared to put it down if security comes along.

Also make sure your feet are on the bench, not hanging over the edge. This seems obvious, but every year you will see about five people fall over because one lost their balance and tipped the bench.

Smoking

There is no smoking inside the tents. Simple as that. If you are caught smoking inside the tent, security will happily throw you out. If you want to smoke, then go to the back of the tent and find the outdoor smoking area. Security will give you a stamp to get back in if necessary, some tents won't bother.

You will sometimes find people using snuff instead of smoking, this is allowed but not particularly common. If you are curious or want to try, just ask someone – most people are happy to share with an interested foreigner.

Toilets

Are there toilets? In a festival devoted to drinking several litres of beer, of course there are! Each tent will have a toilet section, usually located in the back corners of the tents. There will be large signs pointing out the direction, though bear in mind that the male and female toilets are often in different locations. Signs will usually be symbol-based, but you should also look out for *Toiletten* (toilets), *Frauen/Mädls/D* (wom-

en) and *Männer/Jungs/Buam /H* (men).

Unfortunately the toilets are in high demand (unsurprisingly enough) which means that there will be queues waiting to get in. The men's' toilet will be fairly quick, with no line at all to use the *Pissoir* (urinals) and usually a 5 minute wait to use the stalls. The women's', by contrast, will have queues of about 10-20 minutes backed up out into the tent proper.

Money at Oktoberfest

Oktoberfest is an almost entirely cash-based economy, you will have a very difficult time purchasing anything with a credit or debit card. The best approach is to withdraw enough money for your day from an ATM before getting to the festival – although ATMs are present on the grounds they tend to have higher fees than the bank-affiliated ones which can be found closer to the *Hauptbahnhof.*

The official currency of Germany is the Euro, just like much of the European Union. No-one at the festival will take other currencies such as US Dollars or Pounds, however there are a number of money-changing offices scattered around the *Hauptbahnhof* area or in the centre of Munich itself.

How much will it cost?

Oktoberfest is definitely an expensive hobby compared to drinking elsewhere in Munich, but it's also a lot more fun than drinking elsewhere in Munich. You should expect to pay roughly:

- About €11 plus €1-2 for a tip per litre of beer.

- €15-€20 for half a chicken or something equally meaty to soak up the beer

- €5-€10 for the drunken snack you pick up after the tents close will be

- €10 to get yourself there and back on public transport

You need *at least* €100 in cash on you when you go to Oktoberfest, probably a lot more if you are going to buy some souvenirs, go out partying afterwards, or catch a taxi back home.

Tipping

Tipping about 10% is expected in restaurants/bars throughout Germany, and Oktoberfest is no exception. More importantly, your server will get grumpy if you don't tip and is less likely to come back with more drinks – it's therefore in your own best interest to add a bit on top.

There is no hard rule for tipping, the usual approach in the tents is to take the cost, round up by a bit (say a Euro or two for a beer) and then just hand that over. This lets you dump your coins (which don't fit in the lederhosen pockets) and requires less thinking for all involved.

 Mr Maß's words of wisdom

Oktoberfest visits can get very expensive, especially if you are slamming down the beer and eating all the food. Bring a lot of cash, or get ready to walk to the ATMs.

Eating and drinking

Beer!

Beer, beer, the reason we're here! As you would expect at an internationally-renowned festival devoted to drinking beer, the beer is fantastic. Any beer served at Oktoberfest needs to have been brewed within the Munich city limits (ensuring that the festival is local) and needs to conform to the *Reinheitsgebot*. The Reinheitsgebot, or beer purity laws, have been around since 1487 in Munich and state that beer can only be made from barley, hops, and water(yeast was later added to the list). The law has been in force since the middle ages and to this day German beer cannot be made from anything but these four ingredients.

Thanks to these rules, Oktoberfest beer is not only delicious but the next-day hangover is much less painful than an equivalent drinking evening with American or Australian beer. Having said that, the beer is stronger than many are used to (about 6% alcohol) and will be delivered in a one-litre glass known as a *Maß* (pronounced "mahss"). This means that you will be drinking quite a lot of alcohol – regardless of the purity laws, you will have a mighty hangover the next day.

Mr Maß's words of wisdom

Although the Maß is an iconic sign of Oktoberfest, don't try to be clever and steal it. The security guards or police will stop you if you try to take them home – because you aren't hiding the glass as well as you think, drunky.

One of the most important parts of Oktoberfest is, naturally, knowing how to say 'cheers' properly. Hold your glass out above the table, look the other person directly in the eyes (breaking eye contact is a big no-no), say *prost!* and tap the glasses together. *Tap* them, don't smash them, despite the hefty weight a glass Maß breaks surprisingly easily and you will end up with a beer full of glass fragments.

For extra Bavarian points, try clinking glasses, tapping the glass to the table, then taking a drink. This is an excellent opportunity to change your grip on the glass if you need to.

There are a few different types of beer which can be ordered at Oktoberfest. In general, any drink which is not a Helles will need to be ordered from the waiter. Just ask, and they will get back to you with your drink.

In rough order of popularity, the beer-variants are:

Helles

Almost everyone will be drinking *Helles* ("bright or lightly coloured"). Helles is a pale lager, clear and with a low level of bitterness. Easy to drink, highly tasty, *Helles* is the standard Bavarian beer and is what you will get if you just ask for 'a beer'. Oktoberfest Helles a special Helles brew, it needs to follow the Reinheitsgebot and must be brewed within the Munich city limits (this is often the only reason why the major Munich breweries still have facilities within the city).

The beer is *stronger than you are used to*. The average strength is about 6%, thanks to a longstanding tradition that the beer for Oktoberfest be brewed in March and then continue fermenting over several months (due to yet another 1500s law banning beer-brewing during the summer months). This law was repealed quite a long time ago but the strong alcoholic tradition remains.

Radler:

A *Radler* (a 'bicyclist') is a half-half mix of *Helles* and lemonade, known in other countries as a shandy. According to tradition it was invented by an innkeeper who discovered that he did not have enough beer for his cyclist regulars. A quick dilution with lemonade led to a surprisingly popular refreshing drink, and the *Radler* took off from there. The drink itself can be controversial – some love it for the refreshing taste, other hate it for the sweetness of the lemonade.

A *Radler* is a very common drink throughout Germany, particularly on really hot days when people are after something lighter than a full beer.

Exactly as good as it looks

At Oktoberfest it is often used as an 'intermission' drink, a way to break up the beer marathon with something slightly different. Although it is not sold in every tent, you can effectively 'pour your own' by ordering a Helles and a lemonade, drinking half of one and then mixing the rest.

A word of warning: although it doesn't taste like it, the *Radler* is still made with Oktoberfest beer – drinking a radler is the equivalent of downing half a litre of 6% beer.

Dunkles

Dunkles comes from *dunkel*, 'dark', and indeed it is a dark lager. This is the traditional Bavarian style, probably the closest you will come to what was served at the first Oktoberfest. It has a malty flavour (stronger than the normal *Helles*), relatively low bitterness, and often a slightly sweeter after-taste. It tends to be less popular than the other beer options and so some tents may not offer it at all. Despite that it is worth ordering a *Dunkles* at least once, if only to get a better feel for the Oktoberfest tradition.

Alkohol-frei

Non-alcohol drinkers and pregnant women can still enjoy the party, as all tents serve *Alkohol-frei* (alcohol-free) versions of their *Helles* beer. Alcohol-free and normal versions taste roughly the same, and it can be surprisingly difficult to tell the difference. To help people out, the glass will normally come with a little cardboard tag on the handle to distinguish the alcohol-free version from the table-full of beers.

Weißbier

The 'ß' in *Weißbier* is pronounced as 'ss' (and yes, you have just learnt some German). *Weißbier* is instantly recognisable by its cloudy appearance (although filtered versions do exist). Brewed using a mixture of barley and wheat, *Weißbier* has a sweeter and somewhat fruitier flavour than the standard beers.

Although it is found in some tents (most notably in the Weinzelt), this beer is not particularly popular at Oktoberfest. Instead, *Weißbier* really shines as a 'breakfast beer' (yes, beer with breakfast, welcome to Bavaria). If you are out recovering after an Oktoberfest evening, you may want to try the full Bavarian breakfast: *Weißbier*, *Weißwurst* (a white sausage), *Süßer Senf* (sweet mustard), and a *Brez'n*, (the traditional pretzel).

Drinks which aren't beer?

Sometimes you want to enjoy a drink which is, well, not beer. Luckily there are a number of alternatives which you can try out.

Water

Yes, you can get water at Oktoberfest! It's either free or very cheap, also comes in a 1 litre *Maß* glass, and is an exceptionally rare sight indeed. However, don't be afraid to ask: every tent *must* provide water, and legally it has to be the cheapest item on the drinks menu (this is a relatively new change, for quite a long time it was cheaper to drink beer than water).

Even if you pride yourself on being a great drinker, you may still want to mix it up with a 'tactical water' or two during the day. The slower approach can be the difference between enjoying a great party until the tent closes and lying in a pool of your own vomit outside on the grass.

Coffee

Realistically, no-one comes to Oktoberfest for the coffee. However, if you have an unquenchable craving for caffeine, your best option is to go to the Rischart bakery tent located within the rides and stalls section. They sell coffee, cakes, and all of the other bits and pieces you would expect from a bakery/cafe.

Wine

If you don't feel like beer, then you can also get wine at Oktoberfest, however the majority of tents will not sell it at all. Instead, you will have to get a place in the *Weinzelt*, which has a selection of over twenty different wines. The atmosphere in the *Weinzelt* is quite different to the main tents, so you keep this in mind when deciding on a place to drink.

Schnapps

It is possible to find schnapps in various places around Oktoberfest, occasionally in the main tents, more often in the smaller tents or outside bars.

In general, though, you should avoid it. Unlike beer, which takes a while to drink, shots such as schnapps will get you very drunk very quickly – even more so when you are with others who are drinking beer by the maß. Save the shots for another day, and stick with the beer – it's what Oktoberfest is famous for, after all.

Buying a drink

Actually buying a drink is quite easy, the main challenge lies in getting the waiters' attention. The whole process will go as follows:

1) The waiter will come down the aisle, usually carrying 10 glasses and screaming at people to get out of the way. This includes you – if you hear someone blowing a whistle and screaming something like "*Obacht!*" ...move.

2) Normally the waiter will stop and put all of the drinks down at the end of the table, then ask who would like a drink.

3) Say how many drinks you want, either in German (*eins, zwei, drei*), or English (one, two, three), or simply by holding up the right number of fingers (for bonus German points, use your thumb to count 'one').

4) Pass the money to the waiter or up the table via others. Tipping is usually expected, so round up by a euro or two. Either pass exact change or tell the waiter how much money you want to give them (i.e. the cost *plus* tip).

5) They will then pass you your beer (or beers) and change. Congratulations, you have bought a beer at Oktoberfest!

6) If you would like something specific, be it a different drink or food, then you will need to ask the waiter directly. This usually works best when it's quieter and some tents won't sell certain drinks (although they all have to sell water). Specific orders also tend to take longer to arrive, so try not to get impatient.

Oktoberfest tents switched to glass *Maße* rather than stone *Krüge* a while back, mostly because the stone mugs prevented people from seeing whether they were getting short-changed on the amount of beer. The Maß has a line towards the top which is (in theory) the point to which it should be filled. In practice this almost never happens. If the pour is really bad then you can (theoretically) take it

to the waiter's station at the side of the tent to get it topped up. This generally is not worth the effort, and you should just accept that under-poured beers are a long-standing tradition.

Eating (in the tents)

There's a huge amount of food on offer at the *Wiesn*, and unsurprisingly most of it is Bavarian. Stalls outside sell stuff that you can take with you, while inside the tents you can usually get a sit-down meal if you want. Normally the menu disappears at some point, usually onto the floor, but you can order at any time.

If you're sitting **in a tent**, things to look out for are:

Brez'n

A big pretzel, basically. They're baked to be crispy on the outside but soft inside, then it will be liberally sprinkled with large chunks of salt. Brez'n come in two variants: small (think of a hand span or so) and large (about as long as your forearm). Inside the tent you will mostly get the large one, often from a waitress wandering around selling them. If you order a *Brot-zeitbrettl* then your meal will usually come with one or two small brez'n.

Obazda

Brez'n are pretty boring by themselves (it's just salty bread, after all), and so to make life more interesting the Bavarians usually pair them with *Obazda*. Obazda is made from cheese, butter, onion, paprika and beer, all gleefully mixed together and served as a scoop on your plate. There will normally be a sprinkling of red onion or spring onion to add more bite, and often a radish for no apparent reason. Although Obazda is most often found in the *Biergarten*, it is also easy to order in the tents.

Obazda is just a bit too solid to be a dip, so the traditional approach is to rip chunks off the Brez'n, smear the Obazda on with a knife, then scoff them with a beer. If you were a real Bavarian, you'd already have the knife hanging from your *Lederhosen*. You aren't, but the waiter will take pity on you for being a pathetic, unmanly tourist and will give you a butter knife.

The very traditional pairing of Brez'n, Obazda, and radish

Halbes Hendl

Literally half a chicken. On a plate. Sounds simple, yes, but it's amazingly greasy and fatty and it's *exactly* what you want to eat after downing a few litres of beer.

In some of the classier joints you may get a little slice of dried-out lemon, which will be mourning the days long gone when it actually contained lemon juice. It's generally not worth even trying, just eat the chicken.

When you're done, take the little towelette to wipe all the delicious grease from your fingers. Alternatively, do the traditional thing and wipe them off on your lederhosen – the grease adds to the charm.

Kaas-Spatz'n

One of the few options for vegetarians, it consists of melted cheese and roasted onions mixed with *Spatz'n*, a type of Bavarian noodle/dumpling... thing. They are really hard to describe in a way that doesn't annoy all the Germans (seriously, go find a Bavarian and say "what's with these German noodles?") - so just eat it.

Schweinshax'n

A roast pig leg. Well, bits of a roast pigs leg at least. It will be rich and covered in crackling, served with a dark beer-based gravy and a *Knödl* (a big, round, bread-based dumpling). The whole meal is very rich, very filling, and the sheer amount of fatty goodness means it is an amazing base for further drinking.

Sausage options

Bratwurst

Fried sausages! The basic sausage is pork, served as a

Mr Maß's words of wisdom

Real lederhosen should be a bit 'speckig', with grease spots and shiny parts to show that they've been worn in. Newly-bought lederhosen just don't look right –make yours dirty as soon as possible!

pair alongside some sauer-kraut and potatoes. If you get the cheap version, it will be *Bratwurst*, some mustard, and a slice of dry bread.

One thing to watch for is tents serving fried *Weißwurst* later in the day when you have explicitly ordered *Bratwurst*. If your sausage comes in a thick skin that is very difficult to bite through, it's likely a *Weißwurst* - go talk to your waiter about it.

Nürnberger

A variant on the sausage theme are the *Nürnberger*. These sausages are much smaller, about finger-sized, and come in sets of six. As the name suggests, they are originally from Nürn-berg/Nueremberg (and in-deed are a protected geo-graphical product these days - which means that your Nürnberger must have been made in Nuremberg). Though smaller, these sau-sages are usually much crispi-er than the bratwurst and so are often the better choice.

Weißwurst

White sausage! *Weißwurst* are a very uniquely Bavarian meal. Traditionally they were made by the butcher from the random meat cuts lying around from the day before,

which meant that they needed to be eaten quickly before the meat went off and everyone got food poisoning. Nowa-days we have refrigeration, but the tradition remains that *weißwurst* can only be eaten before midday. Most tents will extend the ordering peri-od out to 2pm or so, but you should stick to the midday rule.

These tubes of tradition are boiled, served with sweet mustard, and have to be peeled (or sucked) out of their skin to eat. Strange as this may sound, it's worth trying *weißwurst* at least once - if only for bragging rights.

Sauerkraut

Shredded, pickled cabbage. This is one of those things that people either hate or... well, eat? It's a cultural thing though, so give it a go, if only so you can bitch about it properly.

Brotzeitbrettl

Germans tend to have large lunches and smaller dinners, a direct contrast to the usual US/British way of doing meals. Because dinner is a smaller affair, many people will simply eat *Brotzeit*, a few slices of bread served with a collection of sliced cheese and meats, perhaps a pickle and a radish or two. Traditionally *Brotzeit* is served not on a plate but one a wooden board, known as a *Brotzeitbrettl*. This can, naturally, also be ordered at Oktoberfest, where it will come with a variety of cheese and meaty cold-cuts, some slices of bread or a brez'n or two, and perhaps something vegetable-based. The meal is filling but not hugely fatty, which means it normally isn't enough for a drinking evening – but those looking for a lighter meal may want to give it a try.

Gurke

It's a rare sighting, but sometimes in the tent you will see the highly endangered pickle man. Stereotypically fat and moustached, he wanders through the aisles holding a giant pickle, a bucket containing more of them in the other hand. Despite his lonesome cry of '*Gurke!*' few people want to buy his wares. If you have a spare Euro, brighten up his life by buying a *Gurke*. Actually, buy two, because then you know the second one is fresh.

Your own food

Don't bring your own food. Simple as that. The interior of the tent is basically the same as a restaurant and thus bringing your own food and drinks will get you thrown out if they catch you (i.e. you can probably sneak in some food, but it's risky). Baby formula and food are exempt from this rule, but food for kids will not be allowed.

Eating (outside the tents)

If you're **outside** the tents, or they've just closed, look for:

Mr Maß's words of wisdom

Haxnsemmel is amazing. Nothing more needs to be said.

Haxnsemmel

Haxnsemmel is amazing. Take the leg of a pig, roast it until it is covered in salty crackling, then slice all of the meat off and stick them in a bun. Crackly, greasy, fulfilling any possible need you could have for something salty, fatty, and not-at-all-healthy. This is a fantastic post-drinking

snack and easily the best one to grab when the tents close. Unfortunately everyone else knows this too, so the store will sell out within about ten minutes. If you feel like enjoying this slice of heaven on earth, get it from the stand next to the Hacker tent.

Gebrannte Mandeln

The standard 'sweet' snack, *gebrannte Mandeln* are roasted almonds, usually coated with caramel or some other sort of sugar. The stalls will sell all sorts of different roasted nuts, typically offering almonds (*Mandeln*), hazelnuts (*Haselnüsse*), peanuts (*Erdnüsse*) and walnuts (*Walnüsse*). You will also usually be able to get fairy-floss (*Zuckerwatte*) from the same stores. All of these stalls are easily identified by the distinctive caramel smell, you will

nor-mally smell them long before you see the stall. Snack stalls can be found in both the rides section and the main tent boulevard and make an excellent sugary snack.

Steckerlfisch

Literally a roast fish on a stick. *Steckerlfisch* are more common as a *Biergarten* meal, they can only really be found at the Fischer-Vroni tent during Oktoberfest. You'll find the stall outside the tent (so the smell doesn't get everywhere) with racks of fish on the grill.

Generally you have to buy an entire fish, so be aware that there will be quite a lot to eat. Furthermore the advertised price will be the *cost per 100 g*. A typical fish will weigh over 300g, so keep this in mind lest the fish be much more expensive than you expected. If you are after a smaller portion, try one of the fish-in-a-bun places which lie on the main boulevard.

If you are a fish fan, *Steckerlfish* are an excellent choice, providing some variety from the usual pork- meals.

Almonds, hazelnuts, peanuts, walnuts and candy-floss – there is no lack of sugary food at Oktoberfest

Wiesn-Herzl

Wiesn-Herzl are the little hearts that you see girls wearing around their necks. Made of gingerbread, and decorated with icing, they're a big tradition at Oktoberfest and come with a variety of sayings. The 'traditional' approach is for men to buy them for their sweethearts, which is why the most common sayings are things such as *"Ich liebe Dich"* (I love you), or alterna-tively *"Ich hab'e Dich lieb"* ('I want to say I love you, but that's too serious right now'). You'll also see terms of endearment such as *"Spatzl"* ('little sparrow') or *"I mog di"* ('I like you' – in deep Bavarian dialect). These days a lot are made for people to buy for their friends or themselves, with names or banal things such as *"Grüße* (greetings) *vom Oktoberfest"*

Steckerlfisch are usually sold from stalls outside the tents.

What you actually do with your Wiesn-Herzl is up to you. You can unwrap it from the plastic and eat it – though bear in mind that there is a *lot* of icing sugar in there. Or you can take it home and keep it as a souvenir of your Oktoberfest visit. The Herzl will easily last for decades before going mouldy (though you won't want to eat it after the first few months) and so makes a good long-lasting reminder of your beer-filled trip.

There's a gingerbread heart for almost every need

Rides

Like any good festival, almost half of Oktoberfest is given over to various rides, ranging from the thrill-inducing rollercoasters to the far more relaxed rotating bars. The majority of them are found on the east side of the grounds, while the tents are mostly on the west. Rides will open at 10am on all days except the first Saturday, when they will open at midday. All stalls and rides will close down at midnight on Fridays and Saturdays, at 11:30pm on all other days.

Like any good fair, the rides at Oktoberfest range from the low key to the heart-pounding. Tickets are usually comparatively expensive, which means you'll be need-ing another €50 if you want to cover the majority of the good ones. However you decide to do it, there are a few classics which turn up every year and which you should check out first.

Rollercoasters

The two traditional roller-coasters are the *Olympia Looping* and *Alpina Bahn*. Olympia Looping has been around since 1989 but still draws crowds thanks to the compact 5-loop set up with a maximum speed of almost 100km/h (it's also apparently the largest transportable 5-loop rollercoaster in the world). Alpina Bahn has been around since 1998, rather than loops it favours a series of hill-like rises which focus on providing negative-G hang time.

Olympia-Looping: A classic Oktoberfest rollercoaster

Other rollercoasters can be found on the grounds, the most notable being the *Höllenblitz*, a spinning coaster (i.e. the carts rotate on the vertical axis) which follows a part indoor/part outdoor track.

Thrill rides

Alongside the rollercoasters are the more compact thrill rides. The most obvious of these are the Skyfall and Power Tower II, both 70+ metre-high freefall drop rides which are tall enough to be seen from all over the Wiesn (you can hear the people screaming from a good distance as well). Other classics such as Parkour, Flip Fly and Top Spin offer excitement slightly closer to ground level.

Oktoberfest classics

Some rides have been around for long enough that they have made their way into photo albums across the world. These may not provide the heart-stopping terror of the previous rides, but are well worth the visit.

One of these slightly-less-dramatic yet classic Oktoberfest rides is the *Wellenflieger*, an elevated carousel in which guests take individual chairs, each hung by sturdy chains, and are then flung around

above the heads of nearby patrons.

Another option, which is highly entertaining for both guests and spectators, is the *Teufelsrad*. Groups of ten will try to sit on the flat wheel, which will begin to rotate at steadily increasing speed until one guess after another is launched off the side into the padded walls. Any managing to stay on for too long will be the target of the operators' ropes, which they will use to gently 'fish' people from their precariously balanced position.

Gentler options

There are also a number of slower options which are suitable for smaller children. The most famous of these is probably the *Münchner Rutsch'n*, 15 metre wide and 55 metre long slide which launches kids and adults over a series of humpback curves.

The last option which all should try is the *Riesenrad*, the giant Ferris wheel located to the south end of the festival grounds. Lifting guests over 50 metres in the air, it is perfect for taking birds-eye photos of the entire Oktoberfest – on clear days you can see all the way to the Alps.

The Riesenrad provides a view across the entire Oktoberfest

After the music stops

It was a fantastic party, but eventually it has to end. The last songs will be sung, the last drinks will be drunk or forgotten, and a crowd of people will file out of the tents into the cold autumn air. Now you need to decide what to do next.

Getting home

You're going to be drunk, everyone else will be drunk, tens of thousands of people will be thrown out of the tents at 10:30pm and *all of them* will want to go somewhere. Some will want to go home, some will want to go to a party, and some will want to go vomit in the corner.

What does this mean for you? Know in advance where you want to go and what you want to do. Here are a few general hints which apply in all cases, more specific information can be found on the next pages.

Write down your address. Before you get to the *Wiesn*, write down the name and address of your hotel, the closest train station, or a friendly looking bridge – wherever it is that you want to go. Some hostels will even give you a card with this already printed out. When you find a taxi or helper, just show them the card and they should be able to help.

Asking for help? Speak clearly. Almost everyone speaks English – the older crowd may have difficulty but anyone official or under the age of 30 will have no problems. Just remember to speak slowly and clearly, as strong accents tend to cause problems.

Buy the right ticket. The public transport system works on a ring system, so that you will pay more for each ring you cross. Everything within the inner city can be visited with an *Innenraum* ticket, you will only need extra tickets if you are staying out in the suburbs. Having said this, ticket checks are quite rare in Munich and almost non-existent on trains leaving Oktoberfest – you can take that as you will.

U-Bahn

The subway system is usually the best way to get around the city. There is one station directly next to the Oktoberfest grounds (*Theresienwiese*, on the U4/U5 lines), however it will turn into a chaotic mad-house directly after the tents close. The U4/U5 lines also go through *Schwanthalerhöhe* station, just west of the Wiesn, although all trains going west (i.e. stopping at *Theresienwiese* first) will be jam-packed. The two stations on the U3/U6 line, (*Goetheplatz* and *Poccistrasse*, south of the grounds) are calmer and will not have the overcrowding issue that the U4/U5 lines do.

S-Bahn

The S-bahn is the extended metro system, there are a number of lines which will all converge on a central line running through the middle of the city. This means that all lines will stop at the two stations closest to Oktoberfest, *Hackerbrücke* and the *Hauptbahnhof* (both north of the *Wiesn*). Reaching either of these stations will require a 10-15 minute walk, but have the advantage of being less crowded and faster when trying to get to the outer hotels. In general you just need to follow the crowds walking north past the church, they will make a beeline for the *Hauptbahnhof.*

Taxi

Taxis will flock around the grounds after closing time waiting to pick up people leaving the tents. Keep in mind that all cars (including taxis) are banned from the ring road around the grounds, so you will need to go a bit further out to find a life. Taxi drivers should use the meter, so never bargain on a trip price.

In general taxis will not take you for a short trip or if you look like you are going to vomit. In these situations you should take a rickshaw, which also saves you from the punishing 'cleaning cost' which you will be hit with after throwing up in the taxi.

Rickshaw

Munich has a number of pedal-powered rickshaws, tricycles which can carry two passengers to destinations in the area. Rickshaws are a competitive business, so drivers will often pimp them out with lights, glow-sticks, stereo systems and shiny reflectors. They will almost all have a couple of blankets to keep the passengers warm during the journey.

Mr Maß's words of wisdom

Rickshaws are a great option when you are staying near the festival grounds. Just remember to say something if you are about to vomit.

Rickshaws are a great option to get anywhere within the local area, the drivers are usually university students, extremely fit, speak both English and German, and tend to come from all over the place. Most importantly for Oktoberfest-goers, they will also take people who are completely drunk and close to vomiting (as opposed to normal taxis).

You'll find crowds of rickshaws at the main exits from the Bavaria Ring, especially in the north end beside St. Paul's church.

But I don't want to go home...

The band plays the last song, everyone sings along to Angels or Bergwerk, and then that's it. The tent closes, and you have to leave. But what if you want to keep partying, rather than just going home? Luckily there are a multitude of options around the city which are happy to sell you a drink or two.

Generally the easiest option is simply to follow the crowd, as most people will also be up for a drink or two and will drift towards the late-night bars. Alternatively, you can try and find:

Near the Wiesn: You can wander south on *Ruppertstr.* to check out Substanz, a fairly small indie club which turns into a jam-packed dance hall after 10pm. You can also go west to the Wiesnclub in the Alte Kongresshalle, just behind the Bavaria Statue, which will cost more for entry but has a more Oktoberfest-club feel.

If you don't mind a bit of walking: You can walk east to Sonnenstraße, just next to Sendlinger Tor U-bahn station, and go to Milchbar. It's a fair size and has a good crowd from about 11pm onwards. Alternatively walk north past Hackerbrücke to Neuraum, a much larger club with different rooms for different music tastes

If you don't mind travelling further. Head over to *Kult-fabrik*, Munich's clubbing area. The simplest way to get here is via taxi, but you can also catch the U-bahn from Theresienwiese or the S-bahn from the Hauptbahnhof to Ostbahnhof station.

This is by no means all the options available, there is basically no lack of bars in the area around Theresienwiese. All of them will be dead quiet until 10:45-11:30pm, as the customers will still be getting out of the Oktoberfest tents. Once they do arrive, however, the place will be packed within half an hour. If you have one particular place in mind, try to go directly there so as not to get stuck in the entry line. Most clubs or after-parties will require you to pay for entry, this is rarely more than ten Euro.

Safety

Millions of people visit Oktoberfest each year, many of them are drunk, and many of them pack into crowded tents and streets. Although your aim should be to have fun, you should also keep a few things regarding safety in mind.

Getting drunk

Let's be realistic here: if you are visiting Oktoberfest, there is a good chance that you will be tipsy, drunk, or wasted before you leave. This is perfectly fine, everyone else is drunk and you could say with a fair degree of accuracy that getting drunk is the main aim of the modern Oktoberfest. Having said that, there is a difference between being a proper Oktoberfest drunk and a loser tourist drunk, so keep a few things in mind:

Know your limits. You should already know how much alcohol you can cope with, Oktoberfest is not the place to discover that you actually can't metabolise more than two drinks. Remember that each Maß is roughly three cans of beer and plan accordingly.

Know how to take a break. If you feel it's getting too much, stop drinking for half an hour, have some water, eat something delicious and greasy. You'll feel better *and* you will have eaten some Bavarian food. Win-win!

Don't skol the beer. Especially don't skol it while standing up on a table. Why? Well, (a) if you can't manage the whole thing, people will heckle you all day, (b) even if you do manage it, security will throw you out and (c) you'll probably be too drunk to make it through the day, which would be a waste of a good party.

Don't pick fights. You see it happen, usually between groups of guys, very often tourists. Security will *seriously fuck you up.* Don't pick fights.

Personal safety

You should keep yourself safe. Makes sense, doesn't it? Alongside the advice we just gave (know your limits while you are drinking!) you should also remember:

Don't bring along expensive things. This includes fancy cameras or large amounts of cash. It's not that theft is a major problem (although it does happen) but also that people do get drunk and drop their stuff, then forget to pick it up again. Having said that, if you've lost something, head over to the Service Zentrum basement for the Lost and Found Office.

Don't pick fights with people. Not only are you ruining everyone else's time, but security and the police will come down on you like a tonne of bricks. Two tonnes if you are stupid enough to hit someone with a *Maß* – this is considered assault with a deadly weapon and you will end up in a jail somewhere.

If something goes wrong, then talk to Security. They are usually fluent in several languages, professional in their jobs, and often quite friendly. More importantly, they have a direct line to the organisation group, which means they can get medical help to you very, very quickly indeed.

The '*Service Zentrum*' is located behind Winzerer-Fähndl and Schottenhaml, next to the Bavaria statue. You can spot it from a distance by the red/white balloon floating in the air. The police are headquartered in the building, while the Red Cross runs a treatment area for the duration of the Oktoberfest. If you have a problem, be it medical or otherwise, then it should be your second point of call after Security.

Unfortunately, despite the best efforts of security and police, rape and sexual assault does still occur. If you feel threatened or unsafe, drunk or alone, then go to the 'Sichere Wiesn' service point at the Service Zentrum. They run a security point for women and girls which is open 6pm-1am each day, and 3pm-1am on Saturdays and which offers a variety of services ranging from help getting home to counselling. The security point can also be reached by phone: +49 (0)89 / 50 222 366.

Terrorism

The threat of a terrorist attack is on everyone's minds lately, and the Oktoberfest organisers are no exception. A number of security measures have been implemented in recent years in order to minimise the threat of terrorist attack:

- Entrance to the Wiesn is only possible through the boulevard gates, where police will be checking bags. A fence has been placed around the entire grounds to prevent people sneaking in across the grass – though this fence can be removed in less than a minute to allow rapid evacuation of the grounds.

- Large bags such as luggage or big backpacks are **not allowed**. Smaller bags such as handbags *may* be checked but in general are not a problem. Baby strollers aren't allowed after 6pm, on Saturdays, or on October 3rd (i.e. the main drinking times).

- Entry to the grounds via the *Theresienwiese* U-Bahn station is slightly more roundabout, and there will also be police controls directly at the exit.

- Although it is unlikely to happen, entrances to the Wiesn may be blocked if the area is considered to be too crowded.

What to wear at Oktoberfest

Ask anyone about their impression of Oktoberfest and it's likely they'll think of the outfits, the traditional Bavarian *Tracht*. Although you can find *Tracht* at festivals across all of southern Germany, it is really only Oktoberfest where everyone gets into the spirit of things. It hasn't always been this way – only a few decades ago *Tracht* was seen as terribly conservative and uncool, most people would turn up in jeans. Nowadays the fashion has swung back again and everyone is all in favour of wearing *Tracht* once more.

Most visitors will already have a good idea of how the traditional outfits look. For men, it usually consists of a pair of *Lederhosen* (literally "leather pants", the name says exactly what they are), a checked shirt (usually red or blue), long socks or *Wadl-Wärmer*, and a pair of green/brown leather shoes. For women, it is the *Dirndl*, (the traditional dress, famous from photos), a *Bluse* (a white shirt that goes under the *Dirndl*), and the *Schürze* (the apron that hangs at the front of the *Dirndl*).

Do I have to wear Tracht?

Not at all! There is no dress code at Oktoberfest, no-one will turn you away at the entrance to the park if you aren't wearing the latest Wiesn-fashions. Even locals will happily turn up in a t-shirt and jeans to have a beer or two. The most important thing is to have fun.

The *second* most important thing is also easy: if you don't have proper *Tracht*, don't try and fake it. Don't be one of those clever people thinking "I can just sew straps onto a pair of board-shorts" or "hey, the T-shirt has a **picture** of *Lederhosen*, same-same, right?" No. No it isn't. You will look like an idiot and everyone will have an even worse opinion of tourists than they already do. Just go in jeans. No-one will think anything bad about you and you'll have a great time.

Mr Maß's words of wisdom

If you're going to wear Tracht, wear Tracht. If you're going to wear normal clothes, wear normal clothes. Just don't wear those horrible tourist creations!

Where can I buy Tracht?

So you like the idea of having your own set of Tracht. But where do you go about finding it?

There are three basic approaches you can use for hunting down the perfect outfit. You can grab something cheap and touristy from a local stall, you can get something mid-priced from shopping centres, or you can get something very fancy indeed from the dedicated stores.

Cheaper options

The most typical option for tourists who are staying one or two nights is to pick something up from a small store or stall. These pop up like mushrooms in the area around the *Hauptbahnhof* and *Theresienwiese*, selling mass-produced clothing for relatively cheap prices. These will normally offer entire sets

of clothing (say Lederhosen, shirt, and socks) which saves a lot of time – shoes will always be offered separately though.

If you are simply after a cheap *Dirndl* or *Lederhosen* set which will keep you partying for one night, then these are the best option. Just keep in mind that the quality won't be the best and that the selection of colours/patterns will be fairly limited.

Mid-priced

The mid-priced options are available from the larger clothes stores, they will set aside entire floors with a dizzying array of *Tracht* options. This gives you a good chance of finding your ideal outfit, and the quality will be a step up from the tourist-specials sold around the main station.

Not all clothing stores target the same markets, thus there are differences in the *Tracht* on offer. You will find cheaper versions in the discount stores such as C&A or second-hand stores such as Re-Sales. The more upmarket chains such as Galleria Kaufhof will have pricier but often higher-quality goods.

High-end

If you really want to spend more money on high-end *Tracht*, then you will need to go to one of the specialty stores. The most popular ones here are *Angermaier* (with a store-front just next to the *Viktualienmarkt* in Munich central) and *Steindl Trachtn* (who are located closer to the old *Isartor* city gate). Expect high-quality embroidery and construction for the clothing, but this will come with a correspondingly high cost - very good quality *Tracht* can cost thousands, though you'll find most items are in the low hundreds range.

Outfits for women

As mentioned before, the usual women's' outfit consists of the *Dirndl*, a *Bluse,* and the *Schürze*. You will also see many women wearing *Lederhosen* and a checked shirt, in a similar style to men albeit with a tighter fit. If you're buying from tourist-focused shops such as those near the *Hauptbahnhof,* the entire outfit will come as a set - either as *Dirndl/Bluse/Schürze* or *Lederhosen/Hemd*. Specialist shops which have a wide selection will let you pick and mix different items, this can let you put your ideal outfit together but usually comes with a higher price tag.

Dirndl

The *Dirndl* is the dress that you see in every postcard from Oktoberfest. The *Dirndl* is actually traditional wear across most of southern Germany, to the extent that you will often see people wearing them on Sundays or for weddings. These are usually longer, reaching down to the ankles, and are made with finer material and fancy embroidery. This is usually too formal and conservative for Oktoberfest and so most people will wear a 'party-*Dirndl*' - shorter and made of cheaper material.

There are a few things to look out for when buying a *Dirndl*:

The cut. The cut is specifically designed to maximise your cleavage. This means that it is intended to be worn with a push up bra (and will often look odd when worn with a different type). It is also intended to be very tight around the torso - the ideal fit is one where you can breathe, but not too much.

Cost. The cheapest varieties are made from cotton and should cost you less than €100. Longer versions or ones with more decoration will cost more. Avoid anything made of silk because the beer stains will be a nightmare to clean out.

Ribbons. Many *Dirndls* will come with a ribbon or chain which makes a criss-cross pattern on the front. Although not essential to keep everything together, the empty hooks/eyelets will nonetheless look strange if you forget to include the ribbon. These hooks/eyelets are also usually the first thing to break - check them carefully before you buy.

Bluse

The *Bluse* is the white blouse which goes under the *Dirndl*, it then gives the outfit 'sleeves' and covers up a bit of the otherwise exposed cleavage. It is normally cut very short, thus it covers the upper body but leaves the midriff exposed - this is

normal, the salesman is not ripping you off.

When looking for a *Bluse*:

Don't skip it. Make sure you buy one! The *Dirndl* tends to look quite trashy if you aren't wearing a *Bluse*, and failing to wear one is the equivalent of painting a big "I'm a tourist" sign on your forehead.

There are many styles. *Blusen* come in many different styles. Some are lacy, some are solidly opaque, some are high cut, some are low cut, some have big puffy sleeves and some have only a thing strap. Have a look around and decide which one suits you best.

Why stop with one? Or buy several, as Blusen are usually the cheapest part of the outfit. You can get a basic one for under €30 and even the fancy ones are rarely more than €100.

Schürze

The *Schürze* is the apron which hangs in front of the *Dirndl*. They are normally bought together as a set to ensure that the colours and style match, but you can also pick-and-match here if you want.

There are a few things which you'll need to know when shopping for a *Schürze*:

The length. The length should be just shorter than the Dirndl. Going with a cut that is noticeably shorter is usually considered a style choice, having a *Schürze* that overhangs the *Dirndl* is a fashion faux pas.

Tying the knot. The location of the knot is traditionally meant to tell you the marital status of the woman: left for single, right for taken, in front for a child/virgin, and behind for a widow (or a waitress). Confused? See the illustration below for a better look.

Lederhosen

An alternative which has significantly grown in popularity in recent years is the female version of the *Lederhosen*/shirt combination. Generally the *Lederhosen* are designed with a shorter cut and slightly tighter fit than male versions (which are

The Schürze knot is more complex than you think. Tying the knot on the right hand side is 'taken' – married, dating, or otherwise not interested. Tying it on the left is 'single'. Children and tourists will have the knot centred in the front. Centred at the back is a widow, but is also common on waitresses.

already quite tight). Shirts are made with tighter fits and more curves, as opposed to the fairly baggy male equivalent. They are then worn with stockings and normal shoes – it is almost unheard of to see women with long socks or *wadl-wärmer.*

Lederhosen for women are sold in the same *Tracht* stores as everything else, so just keep an eye out while you are shopping.

Outfits for men

There is less variety in men's' *Tracht* than in women's', as almost everyone will be wearing the same combination of *Lederhosen*, *Hemd*, and socks. Despite this, there are still ways to stand out.

Lederhosen

Lederhosen are the typical leather shorts which you will have seen in every single photo of Oktoberfest, and probably in every second photo of a 'German' in general. Despite the stereotype, *Lederhosen* are very much a southern-Germany thing, particularly as you get towards the Alps. As with *Dirndls*, you will still see people wearing *Lederhosen* on formal occasions or for festivals. Unlike the *Dirndl*, *Lederhosen* are meant to get dirty – a well-used pair should have occasional grease stains and bare patches from use.

Mr Maß's words of wisdom

The old joke goes: A Bavarian woman goes into the doctors' office to talk about her husband's sudden illness. The doctor says that he can't make a proper diagnosis without a urine and stool sample. "Not a problem," replies the woman, "I brought his Lederhosen along."

When looking for a pair of *Lederhosen*, there are a few things to keep in mind:

Styles of Lederhosen. There are two basic types of Leder-

hosen, ending either above the knee or below the knee. Below the knee is considered more formal and is more often seen on older or more conservative people. Shorter, above-the-knee *Lederhosen* are by far the most common.

Cost. Shorter Lederhosen also have the advantage of being cheaper (starting at about €150), although you can easily spend thousands of Euro if you want the finest goat-leather with embroidery.

You don't need to wear the bracers. The Lederhosen will come with bracers which go up over your shoulders. Feel free to take these off if you don't like them – many people just wear the 'pants' part by itself.

They are really tight? Yes, they are tight. Particularly when you first buy a pair, they will be really tight. Over time they stretch to fit you, but this will take a year or two. If the *Lederhosen* are too tight, there is a cord at the back which can be untied to give a few centimetres of extra room – this is usually used after a particularly hefty Bavarian meal.

Hemd (shirt)

There are two sorts of *Hemd* (shirt) which are worn with Lederhosen:

Checked shirts. The most common form is a long-sleeved checked shirt, usually with a red or blue pattern (though you can get green and purple easily too, other colours may take some searching).

White shirts. The more traditional form is a white, V-neck shirt, also long-sleeved but without buttons (i.e. more of a thin pullover than a shirt). They will often have patterns embroidered onto the front. This version is comparatively rare, you are more likely to see it at a village festival.

Both types of shirts can be found in both normal and second hand stores throughout the area. A checked shirt will cost less than €40, white ones may be more expensive.

Socks and Loferl/Wadl-Wärmer

Bavarians realised long ago that there is nothing sexier than shorts and long socks, and so kept this going throughout the centuries. The socks are usually brown or green, and yes, they should be pulled up.

Beyond that, there are a few things to keep an eye out for:

Long socks go with long Lederhosen. Yes, you should pull them up. Ideally they should overlap, so that no skin is actually visible.

Socks will cost less than €20 for a pair. While it is theoretically possible to find second-hand ones, you probably don't want to. Just buy a new pair.

Loferl or *Wadl-Wärmer* are designed with one goal, to warm your *Wadl*. Say what? Meant to go with the short *Lederhosen*, these are basically knitted tubes that will be pulled up to cover your calves, keeping them toasty warm while you're out hiking in the mountains, or drinking. They also come with short socks for your feet. Though you wouldn't expect it, these are quite stretchy, and so even those unmanly types lacking proper Bavarian calf muscles will not have problems with them slipping down. Strangely enough, *Loferl/Wadl-Wärmer* are more expensive than the longer socks (about €20-30 new), despite having less material.

Haferlschuh

Haferlschuh are the traditional shoes, made out of tough leather with the suede turned out:

Do you really need them? Many people don't actually own Haferlschuh, which means that you can easily skip buying this. Simply wear some brown shoes, or even runners – no-one will pay attention to it.

Get the right size. If you buy *Haferlschuh*, **get the right size**. They are made of very solid leather that takes a long time to soften, and you will be wearing them for hours. Nothing quite kills a party mood like massive blisters or the discovery that you are bleeding into your shoes. I can assure you from personal experience that this is Not Fun, so buy the right size! Our table below will help you get an idea on shoe sizes.

Haferlschuh are normally about €60-80 when new, and are in general quite difficult to find second-hand. As mentioned, however, you can often leave these until later.

Mr Maß's words of wisdom

Seriously, get the right shoe size!

Don't know your shoe size? Here's a helpful comparison table

Europe	U.K., Australia	USA, Canada
35	3	3 ½
36	4	4 ½
37	4 ½	5
38	5 ½	6
39	6 ½	7
40	7	7 ½
41	7 ½	8
42	8	8 ½
43	8 ½	9
44	10	10 ½
45	11	11 ½

Some History

Although most people are simply there for the party, it never hurts to know at least a little bit of the history of Oktoberfest. Here's a very quick overview of what has happened throughout the years...

1810

The event which kicked off everything was a wedding party, celebrating the marriage of the Crown Prince of Bavaria, Ludwig the First, to a relatively unimportant Princess known as Therese von Saxe-Hildburghausen. Some horse-mad men in the National Guard proposed that the event be celebrated with a giant party and a horse race, and Ludwig took the idea and went all out. Most of the city attended the celebrations on the 17th of October, drinking and feasting on the field we now know as the *Theresien-wiese*, named after Ludwig's' new bride.

Crown Prince and later King Ludwig was a highly entertaining historical figure. His addiction to all things Greek is responsible for many of Munich's more strikingly Greek-looking buildings. His sense of self-importance brought us the *Walhalla*, a temple in which marble busts of German heroes look upon a statue of King Ludwig with approval. His political skill helped face down the quintessentially German 'Beer Riots of 1844'. And, most importantly, his appreciation of everything female led to the creation of the *Schönheitengalerie* (the Gallery of Beauties) in Munich, an extensive portrait collection of women he wanted to sleep with (and, in many cases, did).

1811

The city of Munich had enjoyed the wedding celebrations so much that they decided to repeat the festival again then next year. Lacking a good reason such as a wedding, the festival centred on an agricultural show in which local farmers could exhibit and sell their prize goods. This agricultural tradition continues to this day, every four years the southern end of the Oktoberfest grounds is set aside for the *Zentral-Landwirtschaftsfest* where people can party and sell cows at the same time.

1813

The party didn't last as long as hoped, because in 1813, only three years after it started, the festival was cancelled. Most of the men in Munich were off fighting for Napoleon at the time and the rest were not in the mood to spend vast amounts of money on a party. This was not a one-off event, the festival has actually been cancelled a further 23 times. This has happened for a variety of reasons, usually due to ongoing wars (as in 1866 and 1870), ongoing outbreaks of disease (such as Cholera epidemics in 1854 and 1873), or in some cases because inflation was running so high that a beer was worth different amounts on different days of the festival (1923 and 1924).

1819

In 1819 the city of Munich officially decides that holding an Oktoberfest festival every year is a good idea. The city takes over the role of organising and funding the celebrations, as before this point it had been funded by independent groups or wealthy donors. From this point the festival begins to more closely resemble the modern-day event, with stalls and rides making a steadily-greater impact on the field.

1850

In 1850 the giant statue of Bavaria is erected in its current location overlooking the *Theresienwiese*. The Greek-style Ruhmeshall (the Hall of Fame) located directly behind the Bavaria is begun in 1850 and finally completed in 1853 – it contains numerous busts of famous Bavarians which are still visible to this day.

1850 is also the year in which the first of the annual Oktoberfest parades occurred. These parades still occur on the first Sunday of Oktoberfest, during which time representatives from all the city's clubs will march through the central city.

1880

Modern technology reached Oktoberfest in 1880 with the installation of the first electric lights throughout the booths and stalls. Although a far cry from the current blaze of neon and LEDs, this was nonetheless the first step in the right direction.

1914 – 1918

The festival was suspended for the duration of the First World War, with the majority of the male population involved in fighting on the Western and Eastern fronts. The pressures of rebuilding the shattered country led to further cancellations in 1919

and 1920, with the Oktoberfest being replaced by the
kleineres Herbstfest, or
'smaller autumn festival'.

1922 – 1923

Post-war reparations de-
manded by Allied powers
combined with a number of
economic mistakes led to
hyperinflation in the German
Weimar Republic. During
1922-1923 the value of a
German Mark changed from
320 Mark per US Dollar to
slightly over four trillion
Marks per US Dollar. The
hyperinflation and general
worthlessness of the currency
led to prices rapidly increasing from day to day. This
prevented any sort of mean-
ingful commerce from being
conducted, and so Oktoberfest was cancelled for both
years.

1939 – 1945

Oktoberfest was cancelled
once more during the Second
World War, lasting from the
initial outbreak of hostilities
through to Germany's final
surrender in 1945. As after
the First World War, the following years only saw a limited celebration in the form of
the *kleineres Herbstfest*.

1950

1950 marks the first year in
which the Munich Oberbür-

germeister officially taps the
first keg in Schottenhamel,
thus starting the whole celebration. To this day Oktoberfest is started with that one
beer and the traditional cry of
O'zapft is!

1980

In one of the worst terrorist
attacks in Germany, a pipe-
bomb detonates near the
main entrance, killing 13 and
injuring over 200. There is a
memorial to this event at the
entrance today, a large bronze
wall with holes indicating
where the shrapnel flew, and
a list of the victims. This af-
termath of this attack led to
significant increases in security around the festival – although it is not readily apparent, the security of the area is
heavily controlled by uni-
formed and undercover po-
lice.

2010

2010 was the 200th anniversary of Oktoberfest, a date
which was celebrated by the
creation of the *Oide Wiesn*
section. The *Oide Wiesn*
offered a relatively comforta-
ble and family-friendly atmosphere with the feel of the
historical Oktoberfest – including olden-style rides, tents
and food. Massively popular,
with over half a million
guests, it was a simple deci-

sion to bring the *Oide Wiesn* back as a semi-regular event.

2011

Although not a major landmark, 2011 is the year in which smoking is officially banned in tents. Technically smoking was already banned, but 2011 marks the point where everyone became Very Serious Indeed about it all.

Useful German Words

Even if you go out of your way to avoid it, you will end up speaking to some Germans during your trip. Most people will speak English, but you can nonetheless entertain everyone with your knowledge of these highly-useful German words.

Aufbrezel'n

Literally to get 'pretzled up', this is neither a contortionist act nor a German sex position. It instead means the act of getting dressed up in a way that looks fancy or swish – such as when wearing a fancy *Dirndl.*

Bavaria (Bayern)

Ah, Bavaria. Bavaria is sometimes described as 'that small country just south-east of Germany', as Bavarians tend to assume that they are far too important to be just one of the 16 German states. As such, they constantly complain about taxes and interference from those meddlers from the rest of Germany. Pretty much every German stereotype which you can think of comes from Bavaria, the *Lederhosen,* the beer, the mountains, etc. Ironically

many of these stereotypes are true, *Lederhosen* and *Dirndls* are often seen in the countryside on weekends, there are many mountains just a short trip outside of Munich, and yes, they will almost always be drinking beer.

Bierleichen

A fantastic German word which literally means "beer corpses". It refers to people who have had far too much beer and then passed out – hence the corpse. You will find most of the *Bierleichen* on the hill to the west of Oktoberfest, though they will be found scattered through the city as well. Munich newspapers usually give a tally of how many *Bierleichen* were dragged off by paramedics as the festival progresses.

Holz vor der Hütte

Literally "wood in front of the hut", this is a standard German slang for large breasts.

Reinheitsgebot

The German Beer Purity Law, a law which dates back many centuries and which is still technically in force today. The original *Reinheitsgebot* was written at a time before the discovery of yeast, and so states that Bavarian beer can only be made from water, barley, and hops. The Reinheitsgebot was replaced by other laws with effectively similar requirements, but many breweries still proudly advertise that they make their beer according to the requirements.

Stimmungskiller

Literally the "mood killer". Having a great time, chatting to everyone, dancing to the *Fliegerlied*, then the guy next to you vomits all over your newly bought *Tracht*? Then starts telling you about his prostate problems? While continuing to vomit? *Stimmungskiller.* Alternatively, the man who sits next to you and explains tax law in great detail while everyone else tries to party. *Stimmungskiller.* Sadly more common in some tents than you would expect.

Tonkrüge

These are the big stone mugs which hold beer, sometimes with a little lid on the top. Oktoberfest switched from *Tonkrüge* to glass *Maß* years ago because everyone was complaining about getting short-changed on beer, (as you can see the fill line with glasses). Those with a taste for tradition can still find *Tonkrüge* in the *Oide Wiesn*.

Trinkgeld

The tip, basically. Unlike other countries such as the United States, waiters get paid a pretty good wage even when providing below-average service. Nonetheless, it is expected that you tip about 10%, if only because it means that the waiter will actually come back later on. Simply take the number they tell you (e.g. €10.50), round up a bit, and say that number (€11) – no calculators required here.

Weißwurstäquator

The imaginary line which divides the noble, manly men of Bavaria and southern Germany from the filthy Northerners, with their strange fish-based diets, oppressive taxation, and inability to speak proper German. Conveniently matching up with the Donau river, this is essentially the line where people stop thinking 'delicious' when looking at *Weisswurst* and begin to think 'what the hell is that?'

Wiesn Gschpusi

Incredibly difficult for foreigners to pronounce, the *Wiesn-Gschpusi* refers to a hook-up that you have during Oktoberfest. Note that it's not just a one night stand, it implies more of a non-official-but-continuous week or so.

Wurst

Sausage... or is it? *Wurst* is a magical word that can be used for anything! See a sausage? That's *die Wurst.* Doing lots of chores around the house? *Rumwurschd'ln* - sausaging around. Boyfriend wanders through life without a plan? *Er wurschdld sich durch* - he just sausages through. Some-thing happens, but you don't give a shit? Meh, *es ist wurst.* There's a lonely shit lying on the road? Yep, that's *Wurst.* Seriously handy.

Zusammen oder getrennt?

Together or separately? When you're paying for stuff at a sit-down place, this is them asking how you want to pay for it all.

Wiesn Songs

The music which you head at Oktoberfest is a mix of old classics and newer hits. Every year a new 'Wiesn-hit' will pop up and be played *ad nauseum* throughout the festival, managing this is fantastic for sales of the song and so marketing plays a heavy role in the choice of final Wiesn-hit. There are a few songs which have been around for years, however, and the most important of these for visitors are *Ein Prosit*, *Fliegerlied*, and *Cowboys und Indianer*.

Ein Prosit

A very old song, the ‚modern' version was composed by Gerhard Jussenhoven and Kurt Elliot back in 1957. You are guaranteed to hear this song multiple times during your visit, it will sometimes be played as often as every 15 minutes in some tents. Because of this, it's by far the easiest to actually remember:

>*Ein Prosit, ein Prosit*

>*Der Gemütlichkeit*

>*Ein Prosit, ein Prosit*

>*Der Gemütlichkeit.*

This short refrain basically translates as "a toast, a toast, to coziness". This is the point where you should meet each other's eyes, clink glasses, and say '*Prost*. The verse will usually repeat several times before going into the final line:

>*OANS ZWOA DREI! G'SUFFA!*

This is Bavarian dialect rather than normal German and simply means "one, two, three, Drink!"

Depending on several things such as the time and the mood of the party, you often get a follow-up from the band:

>*Prost Ihr Säcke!*

Which literally means 'cheers you sacks!' but is really an equivalent of saying 'cheers, you wankers!'

When the band do this, you have to reply:

Prost du Sack!

Again, the equivalent of shouting 'cheers, wanker!'

So ein schöner Tag (Fliegerlied)

This is a surprisingly catchy song, originally developed as a kids' song by Donnikl and then caught on across Germany. It comes with a number of bonus actions that everyone will do while singing along to the chorus – see below for an overview.

Intro:

Ich lieg gern im Gras und schau zum Himmel rauf

(I like to lie in the grass, and watch the sky).

Schaun die ganzen Wolken nicht lustig aus?

(Don't the clouds look funny?)

Und Fliegt ein Flieger vorbei, dann wink ich zu ihm rauf

(And when a plane flies by, I wave up at it)

Und bist du auch noch dabei, dann bin ich super drauf

(And if you're here too, then I feel fantastic.)

Chorus:

Words	Action
Und ich flieg, flieg, flieg, wie ein Flieger	Hands out like wings
(I fly, fly, fly, like a plane)	
bin so stark, stark, stark, wie ein Tiger	Flex those arms like a bodybuilder

(I'm strong, strong, strong like a Tiger!)

und so groß, groß, groß, wie 'ne Giraffe

(and so tall, tall, tall like a giraffe)

so hoch uoh-oh-oh

(So high!)

Und ich spring, spring, spring immer wieder,

(And I jump, jump, jump, keep on jumping)

und ich schwimm, schwimm, schwimm zu dir rüber

(And I swim, swim, swim over to you)

und ich nehm, nehm, nehm dich bei der Hand.

(And I take, take, take you by the hand.)

Weil ich dich mag, und ich sag:

(Because I like you! So I say)

Heut ist so ein schöner Tag - la, la, la, la, la

(today is such a beautiful day...)

Repeat the chorus a few times..

	Stretch as high as you can
	Jumping actions, like a kangaroo
	Swim
	Take the hand of your neighbour
	And jump up and down

Cowboy und Indianer

This is an Oktoberfest classic from Olaf Henning/Mallorca Cowboys which you will hear every night, often several times. Both the song and dance are heavy on the innuendo, which means that both adults and kids will find it entertaining.

Chorus:

Words	Action
Komm hol das Lasso raus, (Come get that lasso out)	Like you're twirling a lasso
wir spielen Cowboy und Indianer, (we're playing cowboys and Indians)	Fingers as pistols (for cowboys) and then feathers behind your head (for Indians)
wir reiten um die Wette (we're riding for the win)	Riding a horse
ohne Rast und ohne Ziel (without rest and without a goal)	Hand like a pillow, then shading your eyes
hast du mich umzingelt werd ich mich ergeben, (and when you've got me surrounded, then I surrender)	Hands up like you're surrendering
stell mich an den Marterpfahl (tie me to the stake)	Hands behind your back like you're tied to the stake
komm hol das Lasso raus, so wie beim ersten Mal. (So get that lasso out, just like our first time)	Feel free to do any sex related action you want here

And then the song continues

So wie ein Cowboy in der Einsamkeit,

(So like a lonely cowboy,)

auf seiner Suche nach Geborgenheit,

(as he searches for safety,)

reite ich immer weiter gegen den Wind,

(I keep riding against the wind,)

so lange bis ich endlich bei dir bin.

(until I'm finally by your side.)

Für dich ist mir kein Weg zu weit,

(For you, no way is too far,)

bei dir vergesse ich die Zeit,

(because with you I forget the time,)

nun bin ich da und ich hör nur wie du sagst...

(now I'm here, and can only hear what you say...)

Sing the Chorus again

So wie ein Cowboy in der fremden Stadt,

(Like a cowboy in a foreign land,)

in der die Angst noch einen Namen hat,

(Where fear still has a name,)

bin wie besessen auf der Suche nach dir,

(I still obsess over finding you,)

jede Gefahr nehme ich ins Visier.

(I'll take any danger, face to face.)

Für dich ist mir kein Weg zu weit,

(For you, no way is too far,)

Denn bei dir vergesse ich die Zeit,

(Because with you I forget the time,)

nun bin ich da und ich hör nur wie du sagst...

(Now I'm here, and can only hear what you say...)

Sing the Chorus twice

Author information

This book is based on a lot of research and many, many (many) visits to Oktoberfest. But don't take it as gospel: feel free to go explore, try something new, and have some fun. Oktoberfest is a giant festival with many hidden surprises, so go and find them! If you find something new and exciting, let me know and we'll add it to the next edition.

About the Author

Chris Harrison moved to Germany many years ago, following a taste for adventure and a love of fine beer. He arrived completely out of his depth, without knowing any of the language, what exactly his new job involved, or even where he would be sleeping on the following night. Only three days later his new colleagues dragged him out to buy *Lederhosen*. Before he knew it, he looked Bavarian enough that tourists wanted to take his photo. Life only got better from there.

Credit for images goes to Chris Harrison as well as Pixaby contributors Akatsuki-7, Alexas_Fotos, AndiCrank, Designerpoint Fcja99, RitaE, and Spurensucher.

Made in the USA
Middletown, DE
12 October 2018